D1590039

JOHN FORD

INTERVIEWS

CONVERSATIONS WITH FILMMAKERS SERIES
PETER BRUNETTE, GENERAL EDITOR

DATE DUE

GAYLORD   PRINTED IN U.S.A.

Courtesy of Photofest

JOHN
FORD

INTERVIEWS

EDITED BY GERALD PEARY,
JENNY LEFCOURT (PARIS),
ASSISTANT EDITOR

UNIVERSITY PRESS OF MISSISSIPPI / JACKSON

www.upress.state.ms.us

09 08 07 06 05 04 03 02 01   4 3 2 1

∞

Library of Congress Cataloging-in-Publication Data

Ford, John, 1894–1973.
    John Ford : interviews / edited by Gerald Peary ; with the assistance of Jenny
    Lefcourt.
        p. cm.—(Conversations with filmmakers series)
        Includes filmography and index.
        ISBN 1-57806-397-3 (alk. paper)—ISBN 1-57806-398-1 (pbk. : alk. paper)
        1. Ford, John, 1894–1973—Interviews.   2. Motion picture producers and
    directors—United States—Interviews.   I. Peary, Gerald.   II. Lefcourt, Jenny.
    III. Title.   IV. Series.

PN1998.3.F65 A5   2001   2001033003

British Library Cataloging-in-Publication Data available

CONTENTS

INTRODUCTION

OTHER AMERICAN FILMMAKERS NEVER had to be persuaded of John Ford's greatness. As the legend goes, young Orson Welles learned to make movies by watching and rewatching *Stagecoach*. Welles's much-quoted mantra was "John Ford, John Ford, and John Ford," the road to *Citizen Kane* and Xanadu. "A John Ford film was a visual gratification," said Alfred Hitchcock, "his method of shooting eloquent in its clarity and apparent simplicity." Frank Capra called Ford "pure great," and Elia Kazan confessed that, even after half-a-dozen films, he studied Ford's oeuvre to learn how to become more cinematic. Ford "taught me to tell it in pictures. . . . Jack taught me to trust long shots," the *On the Waterfront* filmmaker said.

Ford's around-the-world, on-the-record adherents include Jean Renoir, Akira Kurosawa, Ingmar Bergman, François Truffaut, Wim Wenders, Satyajit Ray. Speaking for all of them was Federico Fellini: "When I think of Ford, I sense the smell of barracks, of horses, of gunpowder, . . . the unending trips of his heroes. But, above all, I feel a man who liked motion pictures, who lived for the cinema, who has made out of motion pictures a fairy tale to be told to everyone, but—in the first place—a fairy tale to be lived by himself. . . . For all this I esteem him, I admire him and I love him."

So too does this unabashed Ford freak, who is proud to have edited this anthology. My infatuation started at age eleven, in the summer of 1956, four incandescent matinee days in a row of watching little Debbie being whisked away by renegade Commanches in *The Searchers,* and with John Wayne's rough, big-daddy, Ethan Edwards, coming after. It was my favorite film immediately and, thirty or so mesmerizing screenings later, it remains my favorite. I met Martin Scorsese once, when he was shooting *Taxi Driver,* and for our hour-and-a-half that's all we talked about: *The Searchers, The Searchers,* and how much we adored it. (I've had that equivalent conversation with many others, including—suprisingly?—Native American novelist, Sherman Alexie.)

The Searchers, perhaps the closest we come to "the great American film," is the pinnacle of Ford's cinematic accomplishment. Among other deeds, he made, in my estimation, the best biography film of all time *(Young Mr. Lincoln),* the best war film *(They Were Expendable),* a classic romance *(The Quiet Man),* two of the best literary adaptations *(The Grapes of Wrath, The Long Voyage Home),* many of the most distinguished, thoughtful of westerns *(Stagecoach, My Darling Clementine, Fort Apache, She Wore a Yellow Ribbon, Wagon Master, The Man Who Shot Liberty Valance).*

Ford even produced—how prescient in the 1950s!—a profound, germane "gender-issues" film showing the tragic consequences of intractable male codes *(The Wings of Eagles,* also his most underrated work).

These carefully wrought studio films, filtered through Ford's shimmering personal perspective, and starring his semi-private stock company of actors (Wayne, Victor McLaglen, Maureen O'Hara, Ben Johnson, Ward Bond, John Carradine, Harry Carey, Jr., Olive Carey, John Qualen, Barry Fitzgerald, etc.), became special things indeed, heartfelt and luminous.

Ford was unusually gallant about love, and he took families seriously, particularly impoverished ones, and he had a special reverence for the hard, sacrificial lives of mothers. No American director has made so many pictures so seriously steeped in American history, from the pre-Revolutionary War *(Drums Along the Mohawk)* to multiple tellings of the displacement of Native Americans (including *Cheyenne Autumn),* to stories of World Wars I and II. Here is critic Andrew Sarris's famous description about Ford: "His style has evolved almost miraculously into a double vision of an event in all its vital immediacy and yet also in its ultimate memory image on the horizon of history."

Formally, Ford was a master of mis en scène, of montage (when, rarely, he wished to employ it), of light and shadows, of framing and settings, of melancholy expressionism fused with transcendant romanticism. The closeups are incomparably radiant and soulful; and, as his director pal, Howard Hawks, saw it, nobody in the history of films has been Ford's match composing long shots.

Ford (1895–1973) arrived in Hollywood in 1914 and began directing in 1917, in the silent-era days of World War I; and he worked steadily into the 1960s, through the dissolution of the studio system. He made more than sixty silent films, about 130 movies in all, including a handful of superb documentaries. At points, his talents were recognized and amply rewarded by his peers: he won Academy Awards, including Best Director for *The Informer, The Grapes of Wrath, How Green Was My Valley,* and *The Quiet Man,* and a Best Picture for *How Green Was My Valley.*

But that was then, not now.

Though he's among the great American artists of the century, worthy to be discussed with Faulkner and Pollock and Ellington and Ives, John Ford is, in truth, hardly part of our national consciousness. Entering the new millenium, he is, for the public, a forgotten man. Young people, including film students, haven't seen Ford's movies, and seem uninterested in going back and catching up. Even repertoire movie theatres are hesitant to book Ford revivals. Unlike a Hitchcock series, the films might unspool without benefit of an audience.

The depressing scenario we know too well. Ford movies are "old" movies, many in black and white, and with the casts and crew all dead. Who today cares? And who contemplates, in a Website postmodern world, long-ago American history? Would anyone under fifty be interested in ancient Hollywood genre movies, many of them woefully unfashionable westerns, and all of them unapologetically sentimental? Would a contemporary crowd pay to see corny, creaky John Wayne?

But there's another key point in the disappearance of John Ford: the filmmaker's complicity in his own oblivion, his lifelong insistence that his movies should not be taken seriously as anything more than popular entertainments. An undeniable barrier to Ford's acceptance as a modern master was Ford himself. While other modernists (Fellini, Tarkovsky, Bergman) were elegantly poetic about their art, taking their genius (and interviews) seriously, Ford as a rule loathed journalists and was wary of cooperating in their assignments. He was legendarily monosyllabic, and gruff to those who posed intellectual questions about his works; and the better they knew his films, the more he might make them suffer.

A paradigmatic Ford encounter of the lethal kind was the filmmaker's brief, acerbic meeting in 1970 with Joseph McBride, a precocious critic who would cowrite with Michael Wilmington the brilliant analytic study, *John Ford* (1971). Ford, almost immediately testy, pushed his interviewer off-stride by a seating at his deaf ear, forcing McBride to sacrifice momentum repeating questions. As for Ford's "thoughtful" answers: Ford described his *Seven Women* as "just a job of work," he said of Jean Renoir's films, "I like all of them," and he characterized *The Searchers* as "a good picture. It made a lot of money, and that's the ultimate end."

Just minutes into the Q&A, Ford excused himself. Interview over. "Everybody asks the same questions, all you people," he told McBride, "and I'm sick and tired of answering them, because I don't know the answers. I'm just a hard-nosed, hard-working . . . ex-director, and I'm trying to retire gracefully."

The John Ford Movie Mystery was the title of Andrew Sarris's book about him. The mystery? From whence sprang Ford's mighty film art: poetic, thematic, thick with cross-references movie to movie, undeniably symbolic? How do you connect the marvelous cinema—so emotional, so richly humanist— with the impatient, curmudgeonly man who subverted attempts by others to elucidate them?

"I hate the analysis, the evaluation that others permit themselves to have," Ford told a French interviewer. "I am a peasant, and my pride is to remain one." Though he was a self-taught expert on American history and military affairs, someone who talked comfortably with John Steinbeck and Eugene O'Neill, he came on when he wanted to (which was often) as what he also was: a blue-collar, Irish-Catholic from Maine, who played football in high school and dropped out of college within weeks to head for California.

Why did he make movies? Because, he contended, of the joy of shooting in the open air and sleeping in a tent. What was he most proud of? Not his Oscars: military decorations, being made by Native Americans an honorary chieftain.

Nobody tried harder to break through Ford's veneer than the British critic-turned-filmmaker Lindsay Anderson *(This Sporting Life, O Lucky Man!)*. He corresponded with, and met, Ford on a series of occasions through the years, beginning in the late 1940s when, as an Oxford student, he wrote enlightened essays praising Ford's films. In 1973, he would visit Palm Springs, California, where the filmmaker lay dying.

The exasperating record of their meetings is contained in Anderson's reminiscences, *About John Ford*.

At the best of times, Ford was vaguely friendly, controlling the agenda of the conversations. At his worst, Ford caused Anderson deep hurt because he was so rudely indifferent to Anderson's side of their exchanges. "He doesn't want to be told anything. Not unless he asked," Anderson wrote of Ford in 1952. "I was not interested to meet Ford as . . . a yessing disciple, oohing and aahing over stories which my common sense told me were not true."

In 1957, Anderson encountered Ford again, and once more came away feeling cheated. The result was a telling summation of the perils of interviewing John Ford on one of the filmmaker's bad-mood days: "His defensive barriers were so strong; and one of its effects was infallibly to make one say the wrong things, ask the wrong questions. . . . His technique was brutal, ruthlessly destructive; by lying, by contradicting everything he'd ever said, by effecting not to understand the simplest question, he could reduce one to dispirited impotence."

And yet, that's not the whole story. Filmmaker Peter Bogdanovich, testifying that "my relations with Mr. Ford weren't always as amicable or easy," still managed in 1966 to coax the crotchety old director into a series of lengthy talks which constitute the monumentally important book-length career interview, *John Ford,* and which were utilized in Bogdanovich's masterly documentary, *Directed by John Ford.* And when Lindsay Anderson asked Ford on his deathbed if there's anything he wanted, Ford replied, and sincerely, "Only your friendship."

Yes, there were situations when John Ford acted almost civil, and a few easygoing storytelling days happened in the presence of journalists. The revelation of *John Ford: Interviews* is the pleasant discovery that there were far more times than anyone previously imagined when Ford more or less "opened up," when, on the record, he discussed his life and career in a friendly, communicative fashion.

Begin at the beginning, with Billy Leyser's 1920 meeting with Ford for the *Cleveland News.* No trouble here: the filmmaker offered a meat-and-potatoes description of behind-the-scenes making the silent western, *Marked Men.* But by 1936, after his break-through Oscar-winning film, *The Informer,* Ford was accruing a volatile reputation—for sarcasm on the set and disarming honesty when being queried. The *New York Times*'s Douglas Churchill wrote of Ford, "He is one of the most difficult men in town to interview. Graced with a rich, deep wit, he constantly says things he shouldn't. . . . His comments on actors as a breed would probably inspire one of the most enthusiastic lynchings the West has known." Difficult? The problem here wasn't Ford, refreshingly uninhibited; it was the family-paper timidity of the *Times* faced with what Ford dared say on the record.

Could Ford be cooperative and charming? Consider Emanuel Eisenberg's 1936 *New Theatre* piece, "John Ford: Fighting Irish." Eisenberg had been warned that Ford was deadly busy; Ford was "a non-giver of interviews." Yet, ". . . (W)e sat for almost two hours in an easy, informal, wandering talk . . . and he . . . extended a further visit to come down to the set next week and watch him direct."

That was the happy fate, too, of *Photoplay*'s Howard Sharpe who, also in 1936, took up Ford's invitation to observe a day of shooting for *The Plough and the Stars*. To Sharpe, Ford talked expansively: about the casting of Katharine Hepburn for *Mary of Scotland*, about how he lights the set and about how he researches. Additionally, Ford dropped the pose of a philistine, and admitted, "Usually I take the story and get every line of printed material I can find on the subject. And then I take the boat and simply cruise until I've read it all."

Did Ford have it in for the establishment *New York Times?* In 1939, *Times's* critic, Bosley Crowther, set up an interview and then worried aloud that "Anything might happen, anything might be said by this cantankerous fellow who reputedly eats young actors like pretzels." Nothing was said; Ford clammed up for Crowther, who wrote in frustration: "Conversation was surprisingly difficult, and for an Irishman, Mr. Ford was grimly laconic." The *Times's* Theodore Strauss did no better in 1941, complaining, "It was difficult to make Mr. Ford talk about himself. . . . He spoke little, and less for the record, of the changes that have come over the movie citadel."

The terse *Times* interviews were an omen. There were few encounters by journalists with Ford through the 1940s. Had he shut down? Moving into the 1950s, Ford was most likely to sit for an interview when he'd ventured away from America, to England or Ireland, or if he was visiting Paris, which he embraced nostalgically because of having been there in the War. In the mid-50s, he met twice on record, affably, with the French critic-theorist, Jean Mitry, and also with Bert Miller, writing from Paris for a Swedish magazine.

Back in the U.S., he consented to be quizzed about making *The Grapes of Wrath* by a young American scholar, George Bluestone, for what would become the classic book, *Novels into Film.* (Bluestone, now a retired cinema professor at Boston University, has contributed here an original recollection of his unusual meetings with Ford.) In 1963, Ford talked with Peter Bogdanovich in Monument Valley, on the set of *Cheyenne Autumn*. "I like making pictures, but I don't like talking about them," he said.

However, also in 1964, he was the subject of a remarkable wide-in-scope interview with Bill Libby for *Cosmopolitan*. Libby explained the secret of his unprecedented rapport with Ford: he simply asked the filmmaker to defend westerns. Ford barked, "Is it more intelligent to prefer pictures about sex and crime, sex maniacs, prostitutes and narcotics agents?" Ford's peevishness somehow got him going. Never again would he talk so articulately about western movies: their history, their morality, their appeal.

In 1965, Ford reverted to acrimonious form, amusingly subverting a French TV team which came to film him in LA. Crouching in pajamas on his bed, smoking a cigar, he pretended to have forgotten his early films, changed the subject mid-talk from his movies to Spanish wine, and suddenly stopped the shooting by clapping his hands and declaring, "I've got to have dinner!" In contrast, Ford began 1966 by sitting down at home to another comprehensive talk, reminiscing even about his silent days, with the astute Danish critic, Axel Madsen.

In 1966, Ford also returned to Paris, where he'd been invited for a gala theatrical revival of the 1948 *Fort Apache*. He consented to something totally out of character: he'd set aside some hours each day to meet with representatives of the French press. Although he would never admit it, Ford must have been pleased that so many French knew his films well and were devoted to them.

One by one, the best French critics came and talked to Ford, seventy-one, as he sat up in his hotel bed at the Royal Monceau. He was quite friendly to all, though not always forthcoming about his old pictures. Observed one critic: "As soon as there's talk of one of his films, he scowls and pretends never to have seen it. . . . John Ford hasn't seen John Ford films." But the two press attachés attached to him, future Cannes programmer, Pierre Rissient, and future filmmaker Bertrand Tavernier, realized that things would go better if they introduced the critics not as journalists but as their friends. Sure enough, Ford loosened up and opened up, even having drinks and dinner with his French compatriots and singing aloud songs from his movies.

"Once in a while we gleaned some information," Tavernier said, though it was spread through a host of newspaper interviews. (The best of these—with Eric Leguebé, Michele Mott, Claude-Jean Philippe, Claudine Tavernier, and Bertrand Tavernier—appear in this volume.)

In America, 1968, Ford relaxed and had fun chatting with fellow western director, Burt Kennedy, for *Action,* the magazine of the Directors Guild. In 1969, he made an informal appearance at the University of Southern California, and set his own agenda: he entertained with raucus stories of practical jokes that he and "Duke" Wayne had played on fall-guy actor Ward Bond. In 1971, he returned to USC for another Friars-like night of movie-related anecdotes. It was Ford's seventy-fifth birthday; however, in the next years, his health would fail after he was diagnosed with cancer.

Fortunately, John Ford's last interview, after he had come home from surgery, is one of the best of all time, a true "summing up." It was in 1973 with Walter Wagner for a chapter for *You Must Remember This,* Wagner's 1975 book of oral histories of old-time Hollywood. Ford reached back to proud family sagas, how his own father came from Ireland to fight in the War Between the States. He told at length, and with relish, his favorite story of movie-making: How I Became a Director. And he ended—how else?—with a deathbed, blasphemous denial of his artistry.

"You say someone's called me the greatest poet of the Western saga," Ford said. "I am not a poet, and I don't know what a western saga is. I would say that it is horseshit. I'm just a hardworking, run-of-the-mill director."

Oh? Quoth Ethan in *The Searchers:* "That'll be the day!"

This book could only exist because of the astounding toil of my assistant editor, Jenny Lefcourt, working out of Paris. While writing her Ph.D. on early French cinema for Harvard University, Lefcourt somehow carved out time to track down every Ford interview conducted in France, and to translate them into English so that I could decide among all those most appropriate for this book. The selections made, Lefcourt's efforts continued, as she located the authors and magazines and negotiated rights for all the French selections. I am deeply indebted to her, as should be all Ford historians.

Back in the U.S., Keith Hamel, now a Ph.D. candidate in film at Indiana University, worked as a second assistant editor, helping me with American permissions. I thank Bill Westfall in Boston, Jon Bloom and David Bartholomew in New York, Michael Chaiken in Philadelphia, and Geoffrey MacNab in London for locating hard-to-find library articles. I thank Ted Elrich at the Directors Guild of America for securing permissions for two Ford interviews, and Mike Robinson at Doc Films in Chicago. At the Lilly Library, Indiana University, Bloomington, Indiana, site of the essential John Ford Papers, I was assisted immensely by Sandra Taylor, Curator of Manuscripts, and by librarian Helena Walsh. Dan Ford, John Ford's biographer grandson, very generously allowed me permission to use interviews and clippings in the John Ford Papers at the Lilly Library.

I also thank Pat Collins in Ireland, Klaus Eder in Germany, Jean Roy in France, Peter Cowie, Richard James Havis, and Derek Malcolm in England, and Peter Bogdanovich in New York. And for crucial translations from Swedish and Danish into English, I am grateful to Jan Lumholdt and Ludvig Hertzberg, both of whom are exemplary film critics.

I am thankful, too, for the expert editorial help, and patience, of Seetha Srinivasan and Anne Stascavage of the University Press of Mississippi, and, as ever, to my wonderful friend, Peter Brunette, general editor of the Conversations with Filmmakers Series. Finally, thank you to my university, Suffolk University, for a summer stipend allowing me to visit the amazing Ford collection at Indiana University.

This book is for Amy Geller, with my hope she will watch lots of Ford movies. And a special dedication to the pantheon film critic, Andrew Sarris, whose *American Cinema* led me to John Ford.

CHRONOLOGY

1895   Born John Martin (later, Aloysius) Feeney, Jr., in Cape Elizabeth, Maine, on February 1, the ninth child (three had died) of John Feeney and Barbara Curran.

1898   Feeney family moves to Portland, Maine, 93 Sheridan St., top floor of a New England three-decker. He grows up here.

1912–14 Plays football for Portland High School.

1914   Graduates high school, attends University of Maine, Oreno, for several weeks, drops out. Goes to California to work for filmmaker brother, Francis Feeney, who had changed name to Francis Ford. John Feeney, Jr., becomes Jack Ford.

1914–17 Works with Francis in various capacities, including props, stunt work, acting, assistant directing.

1915   Appears as a Klansman in *The Birth of a Nation.*

1917   Directs first film for Carl Laemmle, *The Tornado,* a two-reel work. Directs first feature, *Straight Shooting,* starring Harry Carey.

1917–21 Directs twenty-one more films starring Harry Carey.

1920   Marries Mary McBride Smith on July 3. Moves to 6860 Odin St., Los Angeles, where they reside for thirty-four years.

1921   Makes first trip as an adult to Ireland. Son, Patrick, is born, April 3.

1922   Daughter, Barbara, is born, December 16.

1923   Changes name to John Ford for direction of Fox film, *Cameo Kirby.*

1924   Directs first major success, the epic western, *The Iron Horse.*

1926   Directs *Three Bad Men,* his forty-third western, but last for thirteen years. Meets Marion Michael Morrison (later, John Wayne).

1927   Travels to Germany. Meets filmmaker F. W. Murnau.

1929   Directs first talking feature, *The Black Watch.*

1930   Directs *Men Without Women,* the first of thirteen-film collaboration with screenwriter, Dudley Nichols.

1933–35 Directs three films starring Will Rogers: *Dr. Bull* (1933), *Judge Priest* (1934), and *Steamboat Round the Bend* (1935).

1935   Directs *The Informer.* Wins first Academy Award for Best Direction, Best Actor for Victor McLaglen.

1936   Directs *The Prisoner of Shark Island,* first of ten-film collaboration with producer Darryl F. Zanuck. Directs *Mary of Scotland* with Katharine Hepburn. They become romantically involved.

1937   Relationship ends with Katharine Hepburn.

1939   Directs three important works: *Drums Along the Mohawk, Young Mr. Lincoln,* and *Stagecoach.* The last, which begins Ford's twenty-three-year collaboration with John Wayne, creates category of "adult western" and wins Best Direction from New York Film Critics.

1940   Directs *The Grapes of Wrath,* Academy Award for Best Direction. Directs *The Long Voyage Home,* Eugene O'Neill's favorite adaptation of his work. Both are collaborations with cinematographer, Gregg Toland.

1941   Directs *How Green Was My Valley,* Academy Award for Best Picture. Appointed Commander John Ford, U.S. Navy Reserves, September 11. In charge of Field Photographic Branch, Pearl Harbor, December 7.

1942   Makes America's first war documentary, *The Battle of Midway,* Academy Award for Best Documentary.

1943   Releases *December 7th,* filming Japanese attack of Pearl Harbor, Academy Award for Best Documentary.

1945   Directs *They Were Expendable,* perhaps best Hollywood battle film about World War II.

1946   Directs *My Darling Clementine.* Forms Argosy Pictures with Merian C. Cooper.

1947   Directs *The Fugitive,* final collaboration with Dudley Nichols.

1948   Directs "cavalry trilogy" opener, *Fort Apache,* starting eleven-film collaboration with screenwriter, Frank S. Nugent.

1949   Directs *She Wore a Yellow Ribbon,* second of "cavalry trilogy," Academy Award for Best Cinematography to Winton C. Hoch.

1950   Directs *Wagon Master* and *Rio Grande,* the latter concluding "cavalry trilogy" and first of three-film coupling of Maureen O'Hara and John Wayne.

1952   Directs *The Quiet Man* in Ireland with Wayne and O'Hara, final Academy Award for Best Direction.

1954   Directs *The Sun Shines Bright,* personal favorite of his films.

1956   Directs *The Searchers,* perhaps his greatest work.

1957   Directs *The Wings of Eagles,* final film with Maureen O'Hara, and perhaps his most underrated work.

1960   Directs *Sergeant Rutledge,* film dealing with racism in the Old West.

1962   Directs *The Man Who Shot Liberty Valance,* final collaboration with John Wayne and his last masterpiece.

1964   Directs *Cheyenne Autumn,* a film dealing with government's ill treatment of Native Americans.

1966   Directs *7 Women,* final work.

1973   Receives American Film Institute's first Life Achievement Award. Receives Medal of Freedom from President Richard M. Nixon, March 31. Dies Palm Springs, California, August 31.

FILMOGRAPHY

Silent films—**John Ford,** director

1917
The Tornado, The Trail of Hate, The Scrapper, The Soul Herder, Cheyenne's Pal, Straight Shooting, The Secret Man, A Marked Man, Bucking Broadway

1918
The Phantom Riders, Wild Women, Thieves' Gold, The Scarlet Drop, Hell Bent, Delirium, A Woman's Fool, Three Mounted Men

1919
Roped, The Fighting Brothers, A Fight for Love, By Indian Post, The Rustlers, Bare Fists, The Gun Packer, Riders of Vengeance, The Last Outlaw, The Outcasts of Poker Flat, The Ace of the Saddle, The Rider of the Law, A Gun Fightin' Gentleman, Marked Men

1920
The Prince of Avenue A, The Girl in No. 29, Hitchin' Posts, Just Pals

1921
The Big Punch, The Freeze Out, The Wallop, Desperate Trails, Action, Sure Fire, Jackie

1922
Little Miss Smiles, Silver Wings (prologue, the rest directed by Edwin Carewe), *Nero* (directed by J. Gordon Edwards and Ford, uncredited), *The Village Blacksmith*

1923
The Face on the Bar-Room Floor, Three Jumps Ahead, Cameo Kirby, North of Hudson Bay, Hoodman Blind

1924
The Iron Horse, Hearts of Oak

1925
Lightnin', Kentucky Pride, The Fighting Heart, Thank You

1926
The Shamrock Handicap, 3 Bad Men, The Blue Eagle

1927
Upstream

1928
Mother Machree, Four Sons, Hangman's House, Napoleon's Barber (sound short), *Riley the Cop*

1929
Strong Boy

Sound Period

THE BLACK WATCH (Fox, 1929)
Director: **John Ford**
Screenplay: James Kevin McGuinness, John Stone, Frank Barber, from the book *King of the Khyber Rifles* by Talbot Mundy
Cast: Victor McLaglen, Myrna Loy, Roy D'Arcy, Pat Somerset, David Rollins, Mitchell Lewis, Walter Long

SALUTE (Fox, 1929)
Director: **John Ford**
Screenplay: James Kevin McGuinness, from a story by Tristram Tupper, John Stone
Cast: George O'Brien, William Janney, Helen Chandler, Stepin Fetchit, Frank Albertson, Joyce Compton, Ward Bond, John Wayne

MEN WITHOUT WOMEN (Fox, 1930)
Director: **John Ford**
Screenplay: Dudley Nichols, from a story by **Ford** and James Kevin McGuinness
Cast: Kenneth MacKenna, Frank Albertson, Paul Page, Pat Somerset, Walter McGrail, Stuart Erwin, Warren Hymer, John Wayne, Robert Parrish

BORN RECKLESS (Fox, 1930)
Director: **John Ford**
Screenplay: Dudley Nichols from the book *Louis Beretti* by Donald Henderson Clarke
Cast: Edmund Lowe, Catherine Dale Owen, Lee Tracy, Marguerite Churchill, Warren Hymer, Pat Somerset, William Harrigan, Frank Albertson

UP THE RIVER (Fox, 1930)
Director: **John Ford**
Screenplay: Maurine Watkins (and **Ford** and William Collier, Sr., uncredited)
Cast: Spencer Tracy, Warren Hymer, Humphrey Bogart, Claire Luce, Joan Lawes, Sharon Lynn, George McFarlane, Gaylord Pendleton, Morgan Wallace, William Collier, Sr.

SEAS BENEATH (Fox, 1931)
Director: **John Ford**
Screenplay: Dudley Nichols, from a story by James Parker, Jr.
Cast: George O'Brien, Marion Lessing, Warren Hymer, William Collier, Sr., John Loder, Walter C. "Judge" Kelly, Henry Victor, Nat Pendleton

THE BRAT (Fox, 1931)
Director: **John Ford**
Screenplay: Sonya Levien, S. N. Behrman, Maude Fulton, from a play by Fulton
Cast: Sally O'Neil, Alan Dinehart, Frank Albertson, Virginia Cherrill, J. Farrel McDonald, William Collier, Sr., Margaret Mann, Ward Bond

ARROWSMITH (Fox, 1931)
Producer: Samuel Goldwyn
Director: **John Ford**
Screenplay: Sidney Howard, from the book by Sinclair Lewis

Cast: Ronald Colman, Helen Hayes, A. E. Anson, Richard Bennett, Claude King, Beulah Bondi, Myrna Loy, Russell Hopton, De Witt Jennings, John Qualen

AIR MAIL (Universal, 1932)
Producer: Carl Laemmle, Jr.
Director: **John Ford**
Screenplay: Dale Van Every, Frank W. "Spig" Wead, from a story by Wead
Cast: Pat O'Brien, Ralph Bellamy, Gloria Stuart, Lillian Bond, Russell Hopton, Slim Summerville, Frank Albertson, Leslie Fenton, David Landau

FLESH (MGM, 1932)
Director: **John Ford**
Screenplay: Leonard Praskins, Edgar Allen Woolf (and William Faulkner, uncredited)
Cast: Wallace Beery, Karen Morley, Ricardo Cortez, Jean Hersholt, John Miljan, Vince Barnett, Herman Bing, Edward Brophy, Ward Bond

PILGRIMAGE (Fox, 1933)
Director: **John Ford**
Screenplay: Philip Klein, Barry Connors, from a story by I. A. R. Wylie
Cast: Henrietta Crosman, Heather Angel, Norman Foster, Marian Nixon, Maurice Murphy, Lucille Laverne, Charley Grapewin, Hedda Hopper

DR. BULL (Fox, 1933)
Director: **John Ford**
Screenplay: Paul Green, from the book *The Last Adam* by James Gould Cozzens
Cast: Will Rogers, Marian Nixon, Berton Churchill, Louise Dresser, Howard Lally, Rochelle Hudson, Vera Allen, Elizabeth Patterson, Ralph Morgan, Andy Devine

THE LOST PATROL (RKO, 1934)
Producer: Merian C. Cooper
Director: **John Ford**
Screenplay: Dudley Nichols, Garrett Fort (and Frank Baker, uncredited), from a story by Philip MacDonald

Cast: Victor McLaglen, Boris Karloff, Wallace Ford, Reginald Denny, J. M. Kerrigan, Billy Bevan, Alan Hale, Brandon Hurst

THE WORLD MOVES ON (1934)
Producer: Winfield Sheehan
Director: **John Ford**
Screenplay: Reginald C. Berkeley
Cast: Madeleine Carroll, Franchot Tone, Lumsden Hare, Raul Roulien, Siegfried Rumann, Louise Dresser, Stepin Fetchit, Reginald Denny, Russell Simpson

JUDGE PRIEST (Fox, 1934)
Producer: Sol Wurtzel
Director: **John Ford**
Screenplay: Dudley Nichols, Lamar Trotti, from stories by Irvin S. Cobb
Cast: Will Rogers, Henry B. Walthall, Tom Brown, Anita Louise, Rochelle Hudson, Berton Churchill, David Landau, Hattie McDaniel, Stepin Fetchit, Charley Grapewin, Francis Ford

THE WHOLE TOWN'S TALKING (Columbia, 1935)
Producer: Lester Cowan
Director: **John Ford**
Screenplay: Jo Swerling, from the book by W. R. Burnett
Cast: Edward G. Robinson, Jean Arthur, Wallace Ford, Arthur Byron, Arthur Hohl, Donald Meek, Paul Harvey, Edward Brophy, J. Farrell MacDonald

THE INFORMER (RKO, 1935)
Associate Producer: Cliff Reid
Director: **John Ford**
Screenplay: Dudley Nichols, from the book by Liam O'Flaherty
Cast: Victor McLaglen, Heather Angel, Preston Foster, Margot Grahame, Wallace Ford, Una O'Connor, J. M. Kerrigan, Joseph Sawyer, Neil Fitzgerald

STEAMBOAT ROUND THE BEND (20th Century-Fox, 1935)
Producer: Sol Wurtzel
Director: **John Ford**
Screenplay: Dudley Nichols, Lamar Trotti, from a story by Ben Lucian Burman

Cast: Will Rogers, Anne Shirley, Eugene Pallette, John McGuire, Stepin Fetchit, Francis Ford, Irvin S. Cobb, Raymond Hatton, Charles Middleton

THE PRISONER OF SHARK ISLAND (20th Century-Fox, 1936)
Producer: Darryl F. Zanuck
Director: **John Ford**
Screenplay: Nunnally Johnson, from the life of Dr. Samuel A. Mudd
Cast: Warner Baxter, Gloria Stuart, Claude Gillingwater, Arthur Byron, O. P. Heggie, Harry Carey, Francis Ford, John Carradine

THE LAST OUTLAW (RKO, 1936)
Associate Producer: Robert Sisk
Director: Christy Cabanne
Screenplay: John Twist, Jack Townley, from a story by **John Ford**, Evelyne Murray Campbell
Cast: Harry Carey, Hoot Gibson, Margaret Callahan, Henry B. Walthall

MARY OF SCOTLAND (RKO, 1936)
Producer: Pandro S. Berman
Director: **John Ford**
Screenplay: Dudley Nichols, from the play by Maxwell Anderson
Cast: Katharine Hepburn, Frederic March, Florence Eldridge, Douglas Walton, John Carradine, Monte Blue, Donald Crisp, Alan Mowbray, Jean Fenwick

THE PLOUGH AND THE STARS (RKO, 1936)
Associate producer: Cliff Reid, Robert Sisk
Director: **John Ford**
Screenplay: Dudley Nichols, from the play by Sean O'Casey
Cast: Barbara Stanwyck, Preston Foster, Barry Fitzgerald, Dennis O'Dea, Eileen Crowe, Arthur Shields, Una O'Connor, J. M. Kerrigan, Bonita Granville

WEE WILLIE WINKIE (20th Century-Fox, 1937)
Producer: Darryl F. Zanuck
Director: **John Ford**
Screenplay: Ernest Pascal, Julian Josephson, from the story by Rudyard Kipling

Cast: Shirley Temple, Victor McLaglen, C. Aubrey Smith, June Lang, Michael Whalen, Cesar Romero, Constance Collier, Douglas Scott, Gavin Muir

THE HURRICANE (Samuel Goldwyn–United Artists, 1937)
Producer: Samuel Goldwyn
Director: **John Ford**
Screenplay: Dudley Nichols (and Ben Hecht, uncredited), from the book by Charles Nordhoff and James Norman Hall, as adapted by Oliver H. P. Garrett
Cast: Dorothy Lamour, Jon Hall, Mary Astor, C. Aubrey Smith, Thomas Mitchell, Raymond Massey, John Carradine, Jerome Cowan, Al Kikume

THE ADVENTURES OF MARCO POLO (Samuel Goldwyn–United Artists, 1938)
Producer: Samuel Goldwyn
Director: Archie Mayo (and **John Ford,** uncredited second unit)
Screenplay: Robert E. Sherwood, from a story by N. A. Pogson
Cast: Gary Cooper, Sigrid Gurie, Basil Rathbone, George Barbier, Binnie Barnes, Alan Hale, H. B. Warner

FOUR MEN AND A PRAYER (20th Century-Fox, 1938)
Producer: Darryl F. Zanuck
Director: **John Ford**
Screenplay: Richard Sherman, Sonya Levien, Walter Ferris (and William Faulkner, uncredited), from the book by David Garth
Cast: Loretta Young, Richard Greene, George Sanders, David Niven, William Henry, C. Aubrey Smith, J. Edward Bromberg, Alan Hale, John Carradine, Reginald Denny, Berton Churchill, Barry Fitzgerald

SUBMARINE PATROL (20th Century-Fox, 1938)
Producer: Darryl F. Zanuck
Director: **John Ford**
Screenplay: Rian James, Darrell Ware, Jack Yellen (and William Faulkner, uncredited), from the book *The Splinter Fleet* by John Milholland
Cast: Richard Greene, Nancy Kelly, Preston Foster, George Bancroft, Slim Summerville, Joan Valerie, John Carradine, Warren Hymer, Ward Bond

STAGECOACH (Walter Wanger–United Artists, 1939)
Producer: Walter Wanger
Director: **John Ford**
Screenplay: Dudley Nichols, from a story by Ernest Haycox
Cast: John Wayne, Claire Trevor, Andy Devine, George Bancroft, John Carradine, Thomas Mitchell, Donald Meek, Berton Churchill, Louise Platt, Tom Tyler, Francis Ford, Chris Pin Martin, Elvira Rios

YOUNG MR. LINCOLN (20th Century-Fox, 1939)
Producer: Darryl F. Zanuck
Director: **John Ford**
Screenplay: Lamar Trotti, based on the life of Abraham Lincoln
Cast: Henry Fonda, Alice Brady, Marjorie Weaver, Eddie Collins, Pauline Moore, Arleen Whelan, Richard Cromwell, Ward Bond, Donald Meek, Milburn Stone, Francis Ford

DRUMS ALONG THE MOHAWK (20th Century-Fox, 1939)
Producer: Darryl F. Zanuck
Director: **John Ford**
Screenplay: Lamar Trotti, Sonya Levien (and uncredited, William Faulkner), from the book by Walter D. Edmonds
Cast: Claudette Colbert, Henry Fonda, Edna May Oliver, Eddie Collins, John Carradine, Dorris Bowdon, Jessie Ralph, Arthur Shields, Robert Lowery, Francis Ford, Ward Bond, Russell Simpson

THE GRAPES OF WRATH (20th Century-Fox, 1940)
Producer: Darryl F. Zanuck
Director: **John Ford**
Screenplay: Nunnally Johnson, from the book by John Steinbeck
Cast: Henry Fonda, Jane Darwell, Charley Grapewin, Russell Simpson, John Carradine, John Qualen, Eddie Quillan, Zeffie Tilbury, Frank Darien, Darryl Hickman

THE LONG VOYAGE HOME (Argosy Pictures–Wanger–United Artists, 1940)
Producer: Walter Wanger
Director: **John Ford**
Screenplay: Dudley Nichols, from one-act plays of Eugene O'Neill

Cast: Thomas Mitchell, John Wayne, Ian Hunter, Barry Fitzgerald, Wilfred Lawson, Mildred Natwick, John Qualen, Ward Bond, Joe Sawyer, Arthur Shields, J. M. Kerrigan

TOBACCO ROAD (20th Century-Fox, 1941)
Producer: Darryl F. Zanuck
Director: **John Ford**
Screenplay: Nunnally Johnson, from the play by Jack Kirkland and the novel by Erskine Caldwell
Cast: Charley Grapewin, Marjorie Rambeau, Gene Tierney, William Tracy, Elizabeth Patterson, Dana Andrews, Slim Summerville, Ward Bond, Grant Mitchell, Russell Simpson

SEX HYGIENE (Audio Productions–U.S. Army, 1941)
Producer: Darryl F. Zanuck
Director: **John Ford**
Cast: Charles Trowbridge, Robert Lowery, George Reeves

HOW GREEN WAS MY VALLEY (20th Century-Fox, 1941)
Producer: Darryl F. Zanuck
Director: **John Ford**
Screenplay: Philip Dunne, from the book by Richard Llewellyn
Cast: Walter Pidgeon, Maureen O'Hara, Roddy McDowall, Donald Crisp, Sara Allgood, Anna Lee, John Loder, Barry Fitzgerald, Patrick Knowles

THE BATTLE OF MIDWAY (U.S. Navy–20th Century-Fox, 1942)
Director: **John Ford**
Narration: **John Ford**, Dudley Nichols, James Kevin McGuinness

TORPEDO SQUADRON (U.S. Navy, 1942)
Director: **John Ford**

DECEMBER 7TH (U.S. Navy, 1943)
Director: Gregg Toland, **John Ford**

WE SAIL AT MIDNIGHT (Crown Film Unit–U.S. Navy, 1943)
Director: **John Ford** (?)
Narration: Clifford Odets

THEY WERE EXPENDABLE (MGM, 1945)
Producer: **John Ford**
Director: **John Ford**
Screenplay: Frank W. "Spig" Wead, from the book by William L. White
Cast: John Wayne, Robert Montgomery, Donna Reed, Jack Holt, Ward Bond, Louis Jean Heydt, Marshall Thompson, Russell Simpson, Leon Ames, Paul Langton, Arthur Walsh, Cameron Mitchell

MY DARLING CLEMENTINE (20th Century-Fox, 1946)
Producer: Samuel G. Engel
Director: **John Ford**
Screenplay: Engel, Winston Miller, from a story by Sam Hellman, based on the book *Wyatt Earp, Frontier Marshal* by Stuart N. Lake
Cast: Henry Fonda, Linda Darnell, Victor Mature, Walter Brennan, Tim Holt, Ward Bond, Cathy Downs, Alan Mowbray, John Ireland, Grant Withers, Jane Darwell, Russell Simpson

THE FUGITIVE (Argosy Pictures-RKO, 1947)
Producer: **John Ford**, Merian C. Cooper
Director: **John Ford**
Screenplay: Dudley Nichols, from the book *The Power and the Glory* by Graham Greene
Cast: Henry Fonda, Dolores Del Rio, Pedro Armendariz, Ward Bond, Leo Carrillo, Chris Pin Martin, Robert Armstrong, John Qualen, J. Carroll Naish

FORT APACHE (Argosy Pictures-RKO, 1948)
Producer: **John Ford**, Merian C. Cooper
Director: **John Ford**
Screenplay: Frank S. Nugent, from a story by James Warner Bellah
Cast: John Wayne, Henry Fonda, Shirley Temple, John Agar, Ward Bond, George O'Brien, Victor McLaglen, Pedro Armendariz, Anna Lee, Guy Kibbee, Grant Withers, Mae Marsh, Irene Rich, Dick Foran

3 GODFATHERS (Argosy Pictures-MGM, 1948)
Producer: **John Ford**, Merian C. Cooper
Director: **John Ford**
Screenplay: Laurence Stallings, Frank Nugent, from a story by Peter B. Kyne

Cast: John Wayne, Pedro Armendariz, Harry Carey, Jr., Ward Bond, Mildred Natwick, Charles Halton, Jane Darwell, Mae Marsh, Guy Kibbee, Dorothy Ford, Ben Johnson

MIGHTY JOE YOUNG (Argosy Pictures-RKO, 1949)
Producer: **John Ford**, Merian C. Cooper
Director: Ernest B. Schoedsack
Screenplay: Ruth Rose, from a story by Cooper
Cast: Terry Moore, Ben Johnson, Robert Armstrong, Frank McHugh, Regis Toomey

SHE WORE A YELLOW RIBBON (Argosy Pictures-RKO, 1949)
Producer: **John Ford**, Merian C. Cooper
Director: **John Ford**
Screenplay: Frank S. Nugent, Laurence Stallings, from a story by James Warner Bellah
Cast: John Wayne, Joanne Dru, John Agar, Ben Johnson, Harry Carey, Jr., Victor McLaglen, Mildred Natwick, George O'Brien, Arthur Shields, Francis Ford, Chief Big Tree

PINKY (20th Century-Fox, 1949)
Producer: Darryl F. Zanuck
Director: Elia Kazan (and, briefly, **John Ford**, uncredited)
Screenplay: Philip Dunne, Dudley Nichols, from the book *Quality* by Cid Rickets Summer
Cast: Jeanne Crain, Ethel Barrymore, William Lundigan, Ethel Waters, Basil Ruysdael

WHEN WILLIE COMES MARCHING HOME (20th Century-Fox, 1950)
Producer: Fred Kohlmar
Director: **John Ford**
Screenplay: Mary Loos, Richard Sale, from a story by Sy Gomberg
Cast: Dan Dailey, Corrine Calvet, Colleen Townsend, Lloyd Corrigan, William Demerest, James Lydon, Evelyn Varden, Mae Marsh, Charles Halton

WAGON MASTER (Argosy Pictures-RKO, 1950)
Producer: **John Ford**, Merian C. Cooper
Director: **John Ford**
Screenplay: Frank S. Nugent, Patrick Ford

Cast: Ben Johnson, Harry Carey, Jr., Joanne Dru, Ward Bond, Charles Kemper, Alan Mowbray, Jane Darwell, Ruth Clifford, Russell Simpson, James Arness

RIO GRANDE (Argosy Pictures–Republic, 1950)
Producer: **John Ford**, Merian C. Cooper
Director: **John Ford**
Screenplay: James Kevin McGuinness, from a story by James Warner Bellah
Cast: John Wayne, Maureen O'Hara, Ben Johnson, Claude Jarman, Jr., Harry Carey, Jr., Chill Wills, J. Carroll Naish, Victor McLaglen, Grant Withers

THIS IS KOREA! (U.S. Navy–Republic, 1951)
Director: **John Ford**
Narration: James Warner Bellah, Frank Nugent, **Ford**

THE QUIET MAN (Argosy Pictures-Republic, 1952)
Producer: **John Ford**, Merian C. Cooper (and Michael Killanin, uncredited)
Director: **John Ford**
Screenplay: Frank S. Nugent, from a story by Maurice Walsh
Cast: John Wayne, Maureen O'Hara, Victor McLaglen, Ward Bond, Arthur Shields, Barry Fitzgerald, Mildred Natwick, Francis Ford, Eileen Crowe

WHAT PRICE GLORY (20th Century-Fox, 1952)
Producer: Sol C. Siegel
Director: **John Ford**
Screenplay: Phoebe and Henry Ephron, from the play by Maxwell Anderson and Laurence Stallings
Cast: James Cagney, Corrine Calvet, Dan Dailey, William Demerest, Craig Hill, Robert Wagner, Marisa Pavan, Casey Adams, James Gleason

THE SUN SHINES BRIGHT (Argosy Pictures-Republic, 1953)
Producer: **John Ford**, Merian C. Cooper
Director: **John Ford**
Screenplay: Laurence Stallings, from stories by Irvin S. Cobb
Cast: Charles Winninger, Arleen Whelan, John Russell, Stepin Fetchit, Russell Simpson, Ludwig Stossel, Francis Ford, Paul Hurst, Grant Withers, Milburn Stone, Dorothy Jordan

MOGAMBO (MGM, 1953)
Producer: Sam Zimbalist
Director: **John Ford**
Screenplay: John Lee Mahin, from the play *Red Dust* by Wilson Collison
Cast: Clark Gable, Ava Gardner, Grace Kelly, Donald Sinden, Philip Stainton, Laurence Naismith, Dennis O'Dea

HONDO (Wayne-Fellows-Warner Brothers, 1954)
Producer: Robert Fellows
Director: John Farrow (and, second-unit, **John Ford,** uncredited)
Screenplay: James Edward Grant, from the book by Louis L'Amour
Cast: John Wayne, Geraldine Page, Ward Bond, Michael Pate, James Arness

THE LONG GRAY LINE (Rota Productions–Columbia, 1955)
Producer: Robert Arthur
Director: **John Ford**
Screenplay: Edward Hope, from the book *Bringing Up the Brass* by Marty Maher, with Nardi Reeder Campion
Cast: Tyrone Power, Maureen O'Hara, Robert Francis, Donald Crisp, Ward Bond, Betsy Palmer, Phil Carey, William Leslie, Harry Carey, Jr., Patrick Wayne

THE RED, WHITE AND BLUE LINE (U.S. Treasury Department–Columbia, 1955)
Director: **John Ford**
Narration: Edward Hope

MISTER ROBERTS (Orange Productions–Warner Brothers, 1955)
Producer: Leland Hayward
Director: **John Ford,** Mervyn LeRoy (and Joshua Logan, uncredited)
Screenplay: Frank Nugent, Joshua Logan, from the play by Logan, Thomas Heggen, and the book by Heggen
Cast: Henry Fonda, Jack Lemmon, James Cagney, William Powell, Ward Bond, Betsy Palmer, Phil Carey, Nick Adams, Harry Carey, Jr., Ken Curtis

ROOKIE OF THE YEAR (Hal Roach Studios, 1955) (Television drama)
Director: **John Ford**
Teleplay: Frank S. Nugent

Cast: Patrick Wayne, Vera Miles, Ward Bond, James Gleason, Willis
Bouchey

THE BAMBOO CROSS (Lewman Ltd.–Revue, 1955) (Television drama)
Producer: William Asher
Director: **John Ford**
Teleplay: Laurence Stallings, from a play by Theophane Lee
Cast: Jane Wyman, Betty Lynn, Soo Yong, Jim Hong, Judy Wong

THE SEARCHERS (C. V. Whitney Pictures–Warner Brothers, 1956)
Producer: Merian C. Cooper, C. V. Whitney
Director: **John Ford**
Screenplay: Frank S. Nugent, from the book by Alan LeMay
Cast: John Wayne, Jeffrey Hunter, Vera Miles, Natalie Wood, Ward Bond,
Hank Worden, Olive Carey, John Qualen, Harry Carey, Jr., Henry Brandon,
Ken Curtis, Dorothy Jordan, Pat Wayne, Lana Wood

THE WINGS OF EAGLES (MGM, 1957)
Producer: Charles Schnee
Director: **John Ford**
Screenplay: Frank Fenton, William Wister Haines, based on the life of Frank
W. "Spig" Wead
Cast: John Wayne, Maureen O'Hara, Dan Dailey, Ward Bond, Ken Curtis,
Edmund Lowe, Kenneth Tobey, Henry O'Neill, Tige Andrews, Mae Marsh,
Willis Bouchey

THE RISING OF THE MOON (Four Province Productions–Warner Brothers,
1957)
Producer: Michael Killanin
Director: **John Ford**
Screenplay: Frank Nugent, from a story by Frank O'Connor and plays by
Michael J. McHugh and Lady Gregory
Cast: Noel Purcell, Cyril Cusack, Jack McGowran, Jimmy O'Dea, Tony
Quinn, Paul Farrell, J. G. Devlin, Eileen Crowe, Maurice Good, Frank Lawton,
Dennis O'Dea

THE GROWLER (U.S. Navy, 1957)
Producer: Mark Armistead
Director: **John Ford**
Cast: Ward Bond, Ken Curtis

GIDEON OF SCOTLAND YARD (Columbia British Productions, 1958)
Producer: Michael Killanin
Director: **John Ford**
Screenplay: T. E. B. Clarke, from the book *Gideon's Day* by J. J. Marric (John Creasey)
Cast: Jack Hawkins, Dianne Foster, Anna Massey, Anna Lee, Cyril Cusack, Andrew Ray, James Hayter, Frank Lawton

THE LAST HURRAH (Columbia, 1958)
Producer: **John Ford**
Director: **John Ford**
Screenplay: Frank S. Nugent, from the book by Edwin O'Connor
Cast: Spencer Tracy, Jeffrey Hunter, Dianne Foster, Pat O'Brien, Basil Rathbone, Donald Crisp, Edward Brophy, John Carradine, Ricardo Cortez, Anna Lee, Wallace Ford, Frank McHugh, Jane Darwell, Edmund Lowe, Ken Curtis, Arthur Walsh

KOREA: BATTLEGROUND FOR LIBERTY (U.S. Department of Defense, 1959)
Producer: **John Ford**, George O'Brien
Director: **John Ford**
Cast: George O'Brien, Kim-Chi Mi, Choi My Ryonk

THE HORSE SOLDIERS (Mirisch Company–United Artists, 1959)
Producer: John Lee Mahin, Martin Rackin
Director: **John Ford**
Screenplay: Mahin, Rackin, from the book by Harold Sinclair
Cast: John Wayne, William Holden, Constance Towers, Althea Gibson, Hoot Gibson, Anna Lee, Russell Simpson, Willis Bouchey, Ken Curtis, Hank Worden, Strother Martin

SERGEANT RUTLEDGE (Ford Productions–Warner Brothers, 1960)
Producer: Patrick Ford, Willis Goldbeck
Director: **John Ford**
Screenplay: Goldbeck, James Warner Bellah

Cast: Jeffrey Hunter, Constance Towers, Woody Strode, Billie Burke, Juano Hernandez, Willis Bouchey, Carleton Young, Mae Marsh

THE COLTER CRAVEN STORY (Revue Productions–MCA, 1960) (Television drama)
Producer: Howard Christie
Director: **John Ford**
Teleplay: Tony Paulson
Cast: Ward Bond, Carleton Young, Frank McGrath, Terry Wilson, John Carradine, Chuck Hayward, Ken Curtis, Anna Lee, Mae Marsh, Willis Bouchey

THE ALAMO (Batjac-United Artists, 1960)
Producer: John Wayne
Direction: John Wayne (and second-unit, **John Ford,** uncredited)
Screenplay: James Edward Grant
Cast: John Wayne, Richard Widmark, Laurence Harvey, Richard Boone, Frankie Avalon, Patrick Wayne, Chill Wills, Linda Cristal, Ken Curtis

TWO RODE TOGETHER (Ford-Shpetner Productions Columbia, 1961)
Producer: Stan Shpetner
Director: **John Ford**
Screenplay: Frank S. Nugent, from the book *Commanche Captives* by Will Cook
Cast: James Stewart, Richard Widmark, Shirley Jones, Linda Cristal, Andy Devine, John McIntire, Paul Birch, Willis Bouchey, Henry Brandon, Harry Carey, Jr., Ken Curtis, Olive Carey, John Qualen, Anna Lee

THE MAN WHO SHOT LIBERTY VALANCE (Ford Productions–Paramount, 1962)
Producer: Willis Goldbeck
Director: **John Ford**
Screenplay: Goldbeck, James Warner Bellah, from a story by Dorothy Johnson
Cast: James Stewart, John Wayne, Vera Miles, Andy Devine, John Qualen, Lee Marvin, Edmond O'Brien, Ken Murray, John Carradine, Carleton Young, Woody Strode, Denver Pyle, Strother Martin, Lee Van Cleef

FLASHING SPIKES (Avista Productions–Revue-MCA, 1962) (Television drama)
Associate producer: Frank Baur
Director: **John Ford**
Teleplay: Jameson Brewer, from a book by Frank O'Rourke
Cast: James Stewart, Jack Warden, Patrick Wayne, Edgar Buchanan, Tige Andrews, Carleton Young, Willis Bouchey, Don Drysdale

HOW THE WEST WAS WON (Cinerama-MGM, 1962)
Producer: Bernard Smith
Director: **John Ford**, George Marshall, Henry Hathaway
Screenplay: James R. Webb, suggested by a series in *Life*
Cast (in Ford sequence, "The Civil War"): George Peppard, Carroll Baker, Russ Tamblyn, Claude Johnson, Andy Devine, Willis Bouchey, Harry Morgan, John Wayne, Raymond Massey

DONOVAN'S REEF (Ford Productions–Paramount, 1963)
Producer: **John Ford**
Director: **John Ford**
Screenplay: Frank Nugent, James Edward Grant, from a story by Edmund Beloin, adapted by James Michener
Cast: John Wayne, Lee Marvin, Cesar Romero, Elizabeth Allen, Jack Warden, Dorothy Lamour, Mike Mazurki, Marcel Dalio, Jacqueline Malouf

CHEYENNE AUTUMN (Ford-Smith Productions-Warner Brothers, 1964)
Producer: Bernard Smith
Director: **John Ford**
Screenplay: James R. Webb (and Patrick Ford, uncredited), from the book by Mari Sandoz
Cast: Richard Widmark, Carroll Baker, James Stewart, Edward G. Robinson, Karl Malden, Sal Mineo, Dolores Del Rio, Ricardo Montalban, Gilbert Roland, Arthur Kennedy, Patrick Wayne, Elizabeth Allen, John Carradine, Victor Jory, Mike Mazurki, Ken Curtis, Harry Carey, Jr., Ben Johnson

YOUNG CASSIDY (Sextant Films–MGM, 1965)
Producer: Robert D. Graff, Robert Emmett Ginna
Director: Jack Cardiff, **John Ford** (two weeks of shooting)
Screenplay: John Whiting, from the book *Mirror in My House* by Sean O'Casey

Cast: Rod Taylor, Maggie Smith, Julie Christie, Flora Robson, Sian Phillips, Michael Redgrave, Dame Edith Evans, Jack MacGowran, T. P. McKenna

7 WOMEN (Ford-Smith Productions-MGM, 1966)
Producer: Bernard Smith
Director: **John Ford**
Screenplay: Janet Green, John McCormick, from a story by Norah Lofts
Cast: Anne Bancroft, Margaret Leighton, Flora Robson, Sue Lyon, Mildred Dunnock, Betty Field, Anna Lee, Eddie Albert, Mike Mazurki, Woody Strode

VIETNAM! VIETNAM! (Ford Productions–USIA, 1972)
Producer: **John Ford**
Direction: Sherman Beck
Screenplay: **John Ford**, Thomas Duggan

JOHN FORD

INTERVIEWS

It's the "Little Things" That Count, Details Essential, Says Jack Ford

BILLY LEYSER/1920

'' EVERY EDITOR IN THE country agrees that *The Three God-fathers,* recently presented to American fiction lovers through the medium of a weekly magazine, was an excellent story with wonderful dramatic possibilities; but . . . these editors overlooked the fact that as a film subject it stood out as a classic with unlimited possibilities.

"And," continued Jack Ford, Universal's great director, who is responsible for the filming of the story under the title of *Marked Men,* "it was the great punches in the story which attracted me. I had Universal buy it, and, of course, it fell to my lot to make a six-reel photoplay out of it with Harry Carey as the star.

"The public has no idea of the work we had to do preparatory to filming the story. It meant building the old-fashioned dance hall on the desert. It meant long tedious days of struggle in the merciless sun on a sand-covered waste. It meant moving men, women, and children from up-to-date hotels to the heart of a deserted country, and making them understand that they were a part of the country and must act accordingly. It meant finding types, the kind that would pass the closest scrutiny of the ever-critical public. And it meant taking a six-weeks-old baby into this fringe of civilization to become the pivot around which the story was woven.

". . . (W)e took the opening reel in a penitentiary. There were no imitation bars, only three imitation prisoners out of the 1,100 convicts shown in the picture, and only one acting guard or 'head screw' shown in the great prison

From the *Cleveland News,* January 27, 1920.

scene. Into this atmosphere I had to take cameramen, lights, and . . . make 1,100 desperate men remember that they were really prisoners in the greatest penitentiary of the West and act accordingly.

"In the second reel I had to find one man who dared risk his life for a thrill, and I found him. His duty was to dash through the railing of a high wooden bridge on a horse and fall sixty feet below in a shallow river. I had six cameramen there to catch the scene from every angle. And I believe it will stand as one of the most daring feats ever performed before a camera.

"I had to find a man who could handle a rifle so well that there could not be a fraction of an inch mistake in his aim, for he shoots at Carey, who is swimming a river, and the bullet is seen to hit just three inches from the star's head.

"And then came a man who knew how to dynamite a safe. There were a lot of amateurs about the country, but they wouldn't do. I had to have a professional, and I borrowed him from the penitentiary. . . . He had served ten of his twenty years, but it seems he hadn't lost the old knack of 'cracking a crib,' and the scene, as a result, is unusually realistic."

These things Jack Ford told me the other day when he spent a day with me between trains on his way to the Coast, (and they) were just a few of the details attendant upon making *Marked Men,* one of the best films Universal has ever produced. . . .

Ford is a stickler for detail. No imitation whiskers are used by people acting under him to show the passing of time. He does not permit them to shave when such a facial effect is needed. In fights there is a real battle, in drinking liquor the real stuff is used, and at a dance the music really plays.

Ford himself becomes a part of the picture. He acts every scene for his principals, and goes through every move for the minor actors in the cast. "In everything I want realism," is Ford's continual cry. . . . For two months he studied the story before outlining any acting. Then he chose his cast, and lastly he spent weeks finding locations. . . . Then came the work, which consumed sixty days, with eight to fourteen hours of untiring acting—and as a result came the masterpiece, *Marked Men.*

The photoplay is being shown this week at the Standard Theater and will serve for those who study the intricate ins and outs of the movies as the finest bit of directing seen in many a day.

Film Capitalizes Stage's Shortcomings, Says Ford

LOS ANGELES EXAMINER/1925

''N OW, ABOUT THE FUTURE of motion pictures. You appreciate, of course, that the industry is still in its infancy.''

John Ford, unsung director of *The Iron Horse,* still the magnet drawing matinee and nightly throngs to Grauman's Hollywood Theater, cleared his throat, adjusted his horn-rimmed spectacles, drew in his chin and tried to look as impressive as the newly elected president of a Chamber of Commerce making his inaugural address.

''Much has been said about art in the making of pictures. We must have bigger and better pictures . . .''

Not a smile betrayed him. He went through the platitudinous harangue with the monotony of a phonograph record.

''The influence of the motion picture is tremendous. It offers the greatest opportunity today. This year will be the greatest . . .''

But in this burlesque of the self-important director, John Ford gave himself away. Going through the recital without a change of expression was eloquent of the game spirit that provides amusement to old and young in *The Iron Horse.* Life to him is an interesting game. Directing pictures provides opportunity for a variety of maneuvers. It's a battle of wits.

''I like outdoor dramas best,'' said Ford. ''On the stage, there is the voice to carry a large share of the drama. In pictures there is no opportunity for the tonal gradations that convey such meaning on the stage. The compensating thrill comes in what the stage lacks—the 'long shots' that bring in a herd

---

From the *Los Angeles Examiner*, May 3, 1925.

of cattle, massive mountain peaks, a chain of waterfalls, or a huge mob of men and women."

"Then you believe the successful picture capitalizes on the limitations of the stage?" was suggested.

The reply sounded like "exactly," but perhaps it was "bologna."

John Ford, The Man behind *The Informer*

DOUGLAS W. CHURCHILL/1936

WITH THE BEST-PICTURE-OF-THE-YEAR discussion engaging both coasts and with the probability that the academy will be forced into naming *The Informer* as the most distinguished offering and John Ford as the outstanding director of the season, the town is beginning to ask questions about both the film and the man who wielded the megaphone.

Known as a "sleeper," one of those pictures that are made and released without even their own lot being aware of it, any vagueness concerning the film is understandable. Not so clear is Hollywood's ignorance of John Ford, born Sean O'Fienne in Portland, Me., who for twenty-two years has been one of the most colorful figures in the industry.

To say that the academy is being "forced" into naming these two is, in a sense, a little unkind. Still, that body never has been noted for going far beyond its ranks when honors were to be awarded. RKO-Radio, where the picture was made, is not a strong academy lot and votes often are cast in that organization according to payrolls. Ford is not an academy member. At least he thinks he isn't. "I think I was for a couple of months," he said, "but when I saw what it looked like, I didn't bother." Aside from the merit of the production and its maker, the academy can hardly overlook the action this week of the New York Film Critics nor the anticipated vote of the Writers' and Actors' Guilds.

Getting Victor McLaglen to play the role of Gypo Nolan was probably the

From the *New York Times,* January 5, 1936. © 1936 by the *New York Times.* Reprinted by permission.

hardest part of the picture for Ford. McLaglen read the book and, after rather ponderous consideration, remained dubious. But, by shrewd salesmanship, Ford convinced him that he was born to the part. "Physically and mentally he was the informer," Ford now says. Then he added, "Just make that 'physically.'"

That line is indicative of Ford. He is one of the most difficult men in town to interview. Graced with a rich, deep wit, he constantly says things he shouldn't and makes remarks about local idols that would result in his exile should they be printed. Separating the discreet from the indiscreet is a reporter's problem. Ford is aware of this and constantly follows some delectable barb, with the admonition "But don't say so." His comments on actors as a breed would probably inspire one of the most enthusiastic lynchings the West has known.

On the set he is kind and considerate—except when he's aroused. Then he resorts to sarcasm and, if this is ineffective, he explodes. A feminine star of some magnitude was in one of his pictures. She began dictating certain phases of the production. Ford stopped her and said, "I was hired to direct this picture. What were you hired for?" Nothing was heard from her during the balance of the film.

The man has a fine contempt for the ostentation and fictitious values of Hollywood. Some fifteen years ago he built a comfortable home near the center of Hollywood and he still lives in it, which is something of a local record. Then his salary was nominal; now he is one of the highest paid directors in the business. He hasn't a swimming pool, but this Christmas he says he "went Hollywood"; he got a ping-pong table for his two children. He thinks Beverly Hills is a very funny place.

He has no intimates among the celebrities of the town. When he wants a social evening, he gets hold of his head gaffer or a couple of carpenters. He likes to associate with reporters providing they don't talk about Hollywood.

He cuts his pictures himself. He says it is the only way for a director to get acceptable material on the screen. At the moment he is at Twentieth Century-Fox making *The Prisoner of Shark Island,* and he is a little worried. He understands that Darryl Zanuck cuts all pictures there. "It has some of the qualities of *The Informer,*" he says, "but it's more Hollywood." He resolves everything into "Hollywood" or "non-Hollywood." He laughs at the town probably more than any other resident.

"A lot of legends have grown up about *The Informer,*" he says. "I'm sorry because they're not true. They say that McLaglen was tricked into doing some of the scenes. That's absurd. Vic is a superb actor. Anything he looks at he can play. He believes in realism on the screen, and he has ideas. That may account for the stories that have been circulated about the sequences in which Gypo was befogged by liquor. But they're untrue. In those shots where he tried to remember Frankie McPhillips's name, Vic didn't learn his lines until the last minute. That put realism into his delivery.

"Vic isn't one of those Trocadero actors. That probably accounts for some of the local attitude. He lives his own life as he wants to, and he hasn't anything to do with the Hollywood crowd. As an actor, he's tops. I hope he gets the academy award. He deserves it.

"As for *The Informer,* Hollywood didn't even know we made it. The newspaper boys around the country pounded away on it and started the public going to see it. They're the ones who made it a financial success."

John Ford: Fighting Irish

EMANUEL EISENBERG/1936

M R . F ORD WASN'T IN to anybody, the information clerk assured
me; the secretary had just told him so. But I had been granted an appoint-
ment the day before. The clerk shrugged and called the secretary again. All
right, I could go in the office, and he pressed a releasing button with an
expression that said: for all the good it'll do you.

The secretary was extremely considerate and greatly concerned for my
sanity. See Mr. Ford *today*? Did I know that he was making tests of Hepburn?
That the filming of *Mary of Scotland* was to begin the day after tomorrow?
She could conceive of no urgency impressive enough for disturbing him.

I walked on the mock-streets of the enclosed studio city. Deserted. What
would I do with the morning? I had made no more than two turns when
suddenly, incredibly, there stood the unobtainable Mr. Ford, chatting leisurely with a couple of men. It was too good, too much like the mechanical
ending of a joke with an over-heavy build-up. I managed to catch his eye; he
winked in recognition; we strolled over to the office; Dudley Nichols soon
joined us; and we sat for almost two hours in an easy, informal, wandering
talk.

I offer the preliminary details of the meeting simply because they are so
representative of the man Ford, his style and his methods. In the middle of
an abnormally busy day he had found time to hang around on the sidewalk
for some gossip. Officially he could be located or approached by no one in
the studio, yet a stranger wandering illegitimately around the lot might

From *New Theatre*, April 1936, 7, 42.

bump into him and attract him away from schedule for a period. He had warned me that I would be lucky if I could talk to him for five consecutive minutes as he went about his work; but the non-giver of interviews found *New Theatre* and its point of view so challenging that he stretched five minutes to 120 and extended a further invitation to come down to the set next week and watch him direct (something Dudley Nichols described as a distinct rarity).

For Ford is Irish and a fighter. He has fought for this way of living within the film industry as he has had to fight for the stories that interested him and the methods he believed in.

Pictures like *The Informer* do not come into existence lightly. To the frantic but still hopeful devoté its appearance—or the appearance of any other film on such a high level—is revelation, oasis and consummation, a sudden reward in the stoical pilgrimage of picture-going; but to one whose eyes have been exposed ever so briefly to the mechanics and finances of Hollywood production, the sheer physical emergence of *The Informer* is a small miracle.

"After all, there's nothing surprising about the difficulty of doing things you yourself believe in in the movies," he said, "when you consider that you're spending someone else's money. And a lot of money. And he wants a lot of profit on it. That's something you're supposed to worry about, too."

"Trouble is, most of them can't imagine what'll make them money outside of what's already been made and what's already made them money before."

"Exactly! That's why it's a constant battle to do something fresh. First they want you to repeat your last picture. You talk 'em down. Then they want you to continue whatever vein you succeeded in with the last picture. You're a comedy director or a spectacle director or a melodrama director. You show 'em you've been each of these in turn, and effectively, too. So they grant you range. Another time they want you to knock out something *another* studio's gone and cleaned up with. Like a market. Got to fight it every time. Never any point where you can really say you have full freedom for your own ideas to go ahead with."

"How do you explain such a crazy setup?" I asked. "By block booking? The star system? The fact that it's first an industry and second an art?"

"I used to blame it largely on the star system," the large genial Irishman told me. "They've got the public so that they want to see one favorite performer in anything at all. But even that's being broken down. You don't think

The Informer went over because of McLaglen, do you? Personally, I doubt it. It was because it was *about* something. I'm no McLaglen fan, you know. And do you know how close *The Informer* came to being a complete flop? It was considered one, you know—until you fellows took it up. You fellows *made* that picture. And that's what the producers are going to learn, are already learning, in fact: there's a new kind of public that wants more honest pictures. They've got to give 'em to 'em."

"How do you think they'll go about it?" I wanted to know. "That is, if they go about it at all."

"Oh, they will," he assured me. "They've got to turn over picture-making into the hands that know it. Combination of author and director running the works: that's the ideal. Like Dudley Nichols and me. Or Riskin and Capra."

The point startled me. "I thought directors were running the works completely now."

Ford snorted, amused. "Oh, yeah? Do you know anything about the way they're trying to break directorial power now? To reduce the director to a man who just tells actors where to stand?" He proceeded to describe a typical procedure at four of the major studios today. The director arrives at nine in the morning. He has not only never been consulted about the script to see whether he likes it or feels fitted to handle it but may not even know what the full story is about. They hand him two pages of straight dialogue or finely calculated action. Within an hour or less he is expected to go to work and complete the assignment the same day, all the participants and equipment being prepared for him without any say or choice on his part. When he leaves at night, he has literally no idea what the next day's work will be.

"And is that how movies are going to be made now?" I asked, incredulous. "Like a Ford car?"

He smiled wryly. "Not if the Screen Directors Guild can help it, boy. Hang around and watch some fireworks."

This Guild, of which Ford is one of the most embattled members, if and when it aligns itself with the Screen Actors Guild and the Screen Writers Guild, a not too distant possibility, will offer the autocratic money interests of the movies the most serious challenge of organization they have known to date.

Talk shifted to *The Informer*. Ford spoke of the great difficulty of persuading the studio that it ought to be tackled at all. He and Nichols arranged to take a fraction of their normal salaries for the sheer excitement of the venture; also, of course, to cut down production cost. Now, of course, the studio takes all the credit for the acclaim and the extraordinary number of second runs and for the Motion Picture Academy award—although Dudley Nichols's formal rejection of the award created considerable ructions. Nichols, it need scarcely be added, is one of the leading spirits of the Screen Writers Guild.

But what about the ending of the picture? I asked. Wasn't that a concession? So many of the criticisms had objected to it. Yes, said Ford, it was a compromise: the plan had been to show Gypo dying alone on the docks, and this had been just a little too much for the producers. Still, the religious ending was so much in keeping with the mystical Irish temperament, Ford maintained, that it was pretty extreme to characterize it as superimposed sentimentality.

How about more such pictures? What were the chances?

"If you're thinking of a general run of social pictures, or even just plain honest ones, it's almost hopeless. The whole financial set-up is against it. What you'll get is an isolated courageous effort here and there. The thing to do is to encourage each man who's trying, the way you fellows have done. Look at Nichols and me. We did *The Informer.* Does that make it any easier to go ahead with O'Casey's *The Plough and the Stars* which we want to do after *Mary of Scotland*? Not for a second. They *may* let us do it as a reward for being good boys. Meanwhile we're fighting to have the Abbey Players imported intact and we're fighting the censors and fighting the so-called financial wizards at ever point."

"Actually tackling social themes would be marvelous, of course," I put in at this point. "But what seems to us almost as important right now is to give the straight version of any aspect of life the movies *do* choose to handle. To avoid distortion and misrepresentation in favor of one interest or another. Don't you think that can be managed *within* this set-up?"

"It can and should!" he exclaimed. "And it's something I always try to do. I remember a few years ago, with the Judge Priest picture, putting in an anti-lynching plea that was one of the most scorching things you ever heard. They happened to cut it, purely for reasons of space, but I enjoyed doing that enormously. And there can be more things like that."

"Then you do believe, as a director, in including your point of view in a picture about things that bother you?"

He looked at me as if to question the necessity of an answer. Then: "What the hell else does a man live for?"

Ford, who is on record as having directed about a hundred pictures, selects *Men Without Women* as his favorite. His desire is to do a film about the men and women workers in the wings of film production; they are the only people in "the industry" who interest him at all. That this is not remotely near being the affectation it may sound like to some is attested by Dudley Nichols, who admires John Ford as one of the most fearless, honest, and gifted men in Hollywood. Ford's house, says Nichols, is the same one he has lived in for fifteen years now; it has never occurred to him to "gold it up" or change it. No movie star or executive may ever be found visiting it. Electricians, property men, and cameramen are the people invariably hanging around—and in this choice of unprominent and unsung companions may very well be found the key to the fighting Irishman's life as a clear-eyed craftsman.

The Star Creators of Hollywood

HOWARD SHARPE / 1936

OUT AT RKO, JUST now, a company is making that symphony of courage and hate and love called *Plough and the Stars,* under the direction of one Sean O'Fienne—a tall and typical Irishman whose beautiful name was Anglicized by an unfeeling Saxon people to Jack Feeney and later changed by himself (he is a simple man) to John Ford. I chose him as the object of my first bombardment of questions because he made *The Informer,* which is the greatest motion picture ever filmed, and because in himself he represents all that is the best of Hollywood and its industry.

The set I walked into was an entire section of Dublin enclosed by a sound stage; from the asphalt studio street to the cobblestones of this Irish square was only a step or two, but the difference in mood was an ocean and eight thousand miles.

. . . "How?" I asked him. "How do you do these things? I want to know how you get your effects, what your technique is, all your methods, whether you work more with camera than with sound, what you do about casting, what you do with a bad script, how you direct a picture—everything."

He didn't even flinch. Sitting there, striking match after match, his hair rumpled by thoughtful fingers, he started, surprisingly, at the beginning.

The routine of his first efforts on any picture is of course dependent on the circumstances, the type of story, the particular stars who are scheduled to work in it.

From *Photoplay,* vol. 50, no. 41, 1936, 14–15, 98–100. Reprinted in Richard Griffith, *The Talkies: Articles and Illustrations from a Great Fan Magazine, 1928–1940.* NY: Dover, 1971, 167, 333–37. Reprinted by permission of Dover Publications, Inc.

"When they gave me *Mary of Scotland* to do, my first thought was of Hepburn," Ford said, with only a trace of brogue in his voice. "She was already set for the role, and it wasn't as if she were just any talented pretty young actress who could be dressed in anything and photographed casually. In that case the primary problem was the star and we had to solve it before we could start on story or script.

"I asked the studio for a print of every picture Katharine had ever made—*Bill of Divorcement, Morning Glory, Little Women, Alice Adams,* all of them—and then I called in the wardrobe department and set men and the story adaptors; together we looked up portraits and old woodcuts of the period costumes Mary, Queen of Scots, wore, and photographs of the rooms in her castle. We sketched gowns and ruffs, we planned backgrounds and settings in rough outline.

"When we had some sort of working basis for departure, we locked ourselves in a projection room and, one each night so long as they lasted, ran the Hepburn pictures. We studied every angle of her strange, sharp face—the chiseled nose, the mouth, the long neck—and then adjusted the sketches to fit her personality. We planned photographic effects, decided how best to light her features and what make-up to use in order to achieve for her a genuine majesty."

He paused to relight the inevitable Ford pipe. "After that was time enough to worry about the story."

"Usually I take the story," he told me, "and get every line of printed material I can find on the subject. And then I take the boat and simply cruise until I've read it all.

"I eat, sleep and drink whatever picture I'm working on—read nothing else, think of nothing else; which is probably the reason the continuity and mood of my products stay at an exact level."

. . . Seated across the stained, round table in the prop Dublin pub—with the tangible mood of fog enclosing the windows and the smell of onions and old beer heavy in the air, he analyzed, in a detached good-natured voice, the elements that make him 1936's ace of directors.

Casting was first, and of supreme importance. "After all," Ford said, sitting back, "you've got to tell your story through the people who portray it. You can have a weak, utterly bad script—and a good cast will turn it into a good picture. I've thwarted more than one handicap of that kind with the aid of two or three really fine actors.

"With the exception of the stars who are signed for parts by the studio in advance, I insist on choosing names for myself. And I spend more time on that task than on any other."

. . . McLaglen is the classic example of this premise. "The studio spent weeks trying to foist better known heavies on me," Ford went on, "but I knew Vic could do the job, and I knew I could handle him exactly as I wanted to. I won in the end—and you saw the performance he gave."

But the strongest forte of Ford is his selection of bit players. You may have noticed in his pictures the constantly recurring faces of ex-celebrities, men and women who once rode the crest of the Hollywood wave and who have, through various adversities, but mostly because of changing public opinion, been relegated to the motion picture backwash. These people he hires for two reasons: one based on objective intelligence, one on mere subjective sentiment.

"From my chair as a director," he said seriously, "I'm able to see that these ex-stars will, after all, give a better performance even in the smallest part than any casual extra would; and it's my contention that the bits in any picture are just as important as the starring role, since they round out the story—complete the atmosphere—make the whole plausible. You've seen, certainly, a good many really fine scenes spoiled suddenly by a background player who is obviously reciting his lines, or blundering awkwardly through his action. I won't have that. A woman walking down a street, while people like Barbara Stanwyck and Preston Foster create a love scene, must walk as well and as naturally as a star would do it, or the effect is lost."

He paused for a moment, and then grinned. "The other, and just as important reason, is that when I was starting in this town those people were kind to me. I want to repay a little of that if it's in my power."

On Ford's private lists are one hundred names—not all of the once great— from which he picks his cast for every picture he directs. Always the same people, always the same results; they know his techniques and his wishes, they are capable and hard-working. To my knowledge it's the only list of its kind in the movie colony.

They help, too, these people, in the building of story. "A good many of the most outstanding incidents I have filmed have been things that members of the company have actually seen or actually done during their lives. For these pictures that deal with the Irish uprising I've looked up former black-and-tan soldiers, former rebels, former onlookers, and given them parts; it adds to the sincerity because in the mass demonstration scenes they remember their own experiences and have real tears in their eyes—and every now and then some extra will offer a suggestion that lends to the authenticity of the production.

"Some of them—Arthur Shields for instance—were really in the Dublin post office when it fell. They were in this pub we've reproduced when the call came to mobilize. I talk with them all informally, and get their opinions, and listen to their anecdotes, and as a result get a better picture."

Which explains, in a measure, some of the superlative effects that have startled you in the multiple John Ford productions you have seen. You remember, of course, the unforgettable scene in *The Informer* where the boy is shot and drops lifeless from a window, while in the agonizing silence his fingernails scratch loose down the wooden sill: one of the extras in the *Informer* company had watched (and heard) that happen at some lost time in his life, and had carried the memory of it through the years until the day came for Ford to use it.

"That particular sequence almost caused me a lot of trouble." The pipe quivered with Ford's laughter. "There was a convention of producers being held at the time, so the rushes were sent up for them to see one afternoon; I asked them what they thought of the scene—and they told me it was all right, not to worry because the sound department could cut out the unfortunate sound of the scratching nails! I'm really afraid I insulted them a little during the next five minutes."

. . . Ford was in Shanghai during the Sino-Japanese war (he recounted this to me as if he were discussing a bridge game) and found time during a particularly cluttered afternoon to see and store away this amusing slice of experience. Shells, as he remembers it, were bursting like exaggerated fireworks over the narrow streets of the old city, and he stood sheltered in a doorway while bits of metal whizzed down at comet speed. Suddenly, around a corner, a plump Chinese nobleman came running—retarded by his heavy silks and splendid trappings, tripping and terrified. His attendants lay dead beside his overturned sedan chair in the street behind; the sky was bursting; and there was no place of refuge.

Then, as an exceptionally huge shell boomed overhead, he stopped short, looked up, and with a quick motion opened his painted umbrella.

He lifted it above his head, took a long breath of relief.

In his new safety he waddled sedately down the sidewalk and out of sight.

Ford shot that scene, translated of course to the mood and circumstance of the Dublin neighborhood, on the afternoon I was there.

. . .[T]his unpretentious Irishman works with a camera as a 1936 Aladdin would work with his lamp; he carries under contract—year after year—one super-cameraman named Joe August, and since the two of them work upon the same basic premise, and since both follow mentally the same artistic groove so far as motion pictures are concerned, between them they manage to achieve a special end that no other director, and no other technician, has managed to reach in all the years Hollywood has been a movie center. Joe is allowed to dream as much as he likes, and insofar as common sense will allow, photograph as he likes—a system which, according to Ford, helps Joe to feel that he really has something to work toward and a responsibility of his own; not deliberate psychology, perhaps, but good.

Sound is of secondary importance to Ford, but nevertheless of great consequence. Forty percent of the time (and this will amaze you) he uses a silent camera without even a mike for moral persuasion on the set.

"In the first place I can talk to my people while a scene is shooting," he explained, "and give them suggestions about expression or movement; as a result I don't have to make so many takes. I've discovered that if you rehearse a scene too much it looks artificial and—well, *rehearsed*.

"Lighting, as a matter of fact, is my strong point. I can take a thoroughly mediocre bit of acting, and build points of shadow around a ray of strong light centered on the principals, and finish with something plausible— anyway that's my one boast. If you'll watch in any of my pictures you'll see the trick I use for special effect: while the stars are running through their lines a diffused glow settles over the background assemblage, which at the same time begins to murmur and then to talk intelligibly. And the louder the voices, the stronger the glow, until the main actors are merely part of a group and the general realism is achieved. It always works. Good technique is to let a spot follow a bit player with an important line or two of dialogue across a shadowed set until his part of the scene is finished too."

So far as the industry—as an industry—is concerned, he has pretty definite opinions. "Just now we're in a commercial *cul de sac*," he complains mildly. "We have time schedules, we are ordered to direct a certain story in a certain way because that's what the middle-west wants and after all the middle-west has all the money. But the profession on the whole is progressing steadily. Actors are getting to be better actors, technicians are learning more about their trade every day, and the success of such simple deathless portraits as 'The Informer' is making it easier for those who have ideals about pictures, to make blasting demands in the interest of their convictions.

"Eventually motion pictures will all be in color, because it's a success and because it's a natural medium. And we'll go out to a Maine fishing port or to an Iowa hill and employ ordinary American citizens we find living and working there, and we'll plan a little story, and we'll photograph the scene and the people. That's all pictures should do anyway, and it'll be enough."

Agree with him, or not; but in his very definite statement you must discover the essence of his personality, both as a man and as a director. Simplicity, real sincerity, hatred of ostentation: greatness.

The Rebels, If They Stay Up This Time, Won't Be Sorry for Hollywood's Trouble

MICHEL MOK/1939

JOHN FORD AND DUDLEY Nichols, the iconoclasts who dared to make *The Informer,* a movie that cost only $218,000 (about one-tenth the expense of the usual super-super) and yet earned scads of money, are up to their old tricks. They've finished a new one, *Stagecoach,* at a total outlay of $250,000.

"In Hollywood," said Mr. Ford, the director, "that's considered the price of a good cigar."

"We're all set," said Mr. Nichols, the scenarist, "to revolutionize the industry again."

A few years ago the Messrs. Ford and Nichols created a sensation by consuming three weeks and less than a quarter million in turning out their masterful, forthright screen version of Liam O'Flaherty's saga of Gypo Nolan, the Judas of the Dublin slums.

The picture, you remember, was an artistic and financial success. Critics predicted that it would mark the end of elaborate, insipid screen slush, start a vogue for simple, direct, intelligent film drama. The "revolution" raged— and died—in the movie columns. The producers continued to crank out the same old elaborate, insipid slush.

"Yes, sir, comes another revolution," said Mr. Ford, "provided, of course, that the picture is ever released."

"We're particularly attached to this one," said Mr. Nichols, "because it violates all the censorial canons."

"There's not a single respectable character in the cast," said Mr. Ford. "The leading man has killed three guys."

"The leading woman is a prostitute," said Mr. Nichols.

"There's a banker in it who robs his own bank," said Mr. Ford.

"And don't forget the pregnant woman who faints," said Mr. Nichols.

"Or the fellow who gets violently ill," said Mr. Ford.

This pleasant opus, the members of the writer-director team explained, is based on "Stage to Lordsburg," a short story by Ernest Haycox. Conceived in the *"Boule de Suif"*-*"Grand Hotel"* tradition, it shows the experiences of eight people accidentally thrown together on a stagecoach ride from Ronto, Ariz., to Lordsburg, N.M.

"It's a simple, intimate little thing," said Mr. Ford. "It isn't even colossal in a small way. It's completely devoid of what the reviewers call 'great directorial touches.' "

"You needn't look for any great writing, either," said Mr. Nichols. "I wrote the plainest kind of dialogue—just the way those guys and gals talk without those sudden, inexplicable flights of poetry in the conversation."

Mr. Ford, whose real name is Sean O'Fienne, and Mr. Nichols, whose real name is Dudley Nichols, have come East for a holiday.

Ford, who will spend his vacation in his native, Maine, is a fellow with a huge, grayish face, thin grayish hair, rumpled gray clothes, horn-rimmed specs and an unfragrant pipe. Mr. Nichols, who used to be a reporter for the old *Evening Post* and *The World,* is tall and slim, with a pink aquiline face and a maestro mop of prematurely gray hair.

"It would be a good thing," said Mr. Ford, "if the producers would get into the habit of making inexpensive pictures. They could turn out twelve films like *Stagecoach* in a year instead of two like *Marie Antoinette.* Think of the work such a policy would give to the people out there. Conditions are awful. Do you realize that an extra, who makes from $7.50 to $11 a day, gets an average of two days' work a month?"

"It would be swell, too, from another point of view," said Mr. Nichols. "With a smaller investment, the producers wouldn't need to please such huge masses of people and watch their P's and Q's so carefully. The old bromide that money talks doesn't hold in Hollywood. In the movies, a million dollars can't raise its voice."

A great many horses were used in *Stagecoach,* and Mr. Ford was proud of the fact that not one of the animals was injured on location.

"The S.P.C.A.," he said, "watched us every minute, and a good thing, too. They raised all kinds of hell with Darryl Zanuck for what was supposed to have happened to the horses in *Jesse James.* The only creature hurt in making our picture was a press agent who got in the way of a posse. Fortunately, there's no society for the prevention of cruelty to press agents."

This reminded Mr. Ford of an incident that occurred on location during the filming of a picture he directed a couple of years ago.

"We were shooting in the desert near Yuma, Ariz.," he said. "It was about 150 in the shade, and not a day went by that some actor, cameraman, or electrician didn't keel over from the heat.

"That made for a lot of delay, and the producer, in his air-cooled Hollywood office, was frothing at the mouth with rage. Day after day he sent us furious wires. We ignored them. Finally, he decided to come out and see for himself what was up. He arrived by plane in a complete tropical outfit, pith helmet and all.

"The moment he blew into town he sent for me, but I was busy in the cutting room and couldn't go to the hotel until twenty minutes later. When I got there, the producer had disappeared. They'd taken him to the hospital. Yep. Heat prostration."

John Ford Wants It Real

FRANK DAUGHERTY/1941

JOHN FORD HAS WORKED in motion pictures for thirty years. A list merely of the titles of his "hit" pictures would take several long paragraphs. But consider some of the pictures he has directed in the past two years, beginning with *Young Mr. Lincoln,* running through *Stagecoach, Drums Along the Mohawk, The Grapes of Wrath, The Long Voyage Home,* and now, *Tobacco Road.*

I am not sure that any director in Hollywood can show a comparable group of pictures directed in so short a time; and perhaps only Frank Capra has directed pictures that even compare to them, directed over a much longer period.

John Ford's position in Hollywood is as secure as anyone's could be; yet he is almost the antithesis of all that Hollywood stands for to the public generally and to the casual visitor to the place. He has lived with his family in the same house in the center of Hollywood for more than twenty years. He has never been inside a Hollywood night club. Except Henry Fonda, with whom he became acquainted when both were working on *Young Mr. Lincoln,* he counts few stars among his close personal friends. His intimates, constant visitors to his home, fellow travelers with him on his yacht, are apt to be technicians on his pictures, bit players, a writer or two.

"Nearly everyone," he says, "wants to write about the thing he knows nothing about. The story of Hollywood has never been told. The real people in Hollywood walk around the streets, the studios, and the sets by the hundreds, and no one pays any attention to them. There are more stories to the square foot in Hollywood than in any other place on earth, I believe; there are more interesting and real people here. There is more drama, and comedy—and tragedy, too . . .''

He is attracted almost sentimentally to the problems of the underprivileged: but his pictures never preach, never try with sermons to make you appreciative of the problem. He presents it cinematically, and lets you draw your own conclusions. He laughs a little today when you ask him if he has joined the ranks of the social reformers.

"You're judging me by two or three pictures," he answers. "Twenty years ago people asked me if I was always going to direct westerns, because I made a couple of dozen westerns. Later I was called a comedy director because I directed comedies. When some of my pictures came along with tragic endings, people said I directed only somber subjects. Now they say I am trying to get S.S. into them."

"S.S.?"

"Social significance. Let 'em find it there if they want to. But I don't spend any time looking for it myself. When I make a picture, I try to find people I like in situations that I think are dramatic. The 'oakies' were dramatic. So were those O'Neill characters in *The Long Voyage Home.* So were those people in the stagecoach going to Lordsburg through the Apache country. That's all there is to it . . .''

John Ford, like Frank Capra, has worked out his best pictures with a single writer—in this case, Dudley Nichols. It was Nichols who turned out the scripts for *Stagecoach, The Hurricane, The Informer, The Plough and the Stars, The Long Voyage Home.* Nunnally Johnson did his scripts for *The Grapes of Wrath* and *Tobacco Road.*

"I've got a whole lot of respect for the people who go to see motion pictures," John Ford says. "I think we ought to make pictures in their language."

New York Close-Up

TEX McCRARY AND JINX FALKENBERG/1952

LIKE ERNEST HEMINGWAY, REAR Admiral "Jack" Ford has tried to live up to the fiction he has created or translated onto film—and has many a scar to prove how hard he tried:

He squeezes two foam-rubber bones in his left hand while relaxing—therapy for atrophy of the muscles in that arm, souvenir of a machine-gun bullet he picked up in the Battle of Midway.

He wears sun glasses even indoors in New York—partial coverup for an almost useless left eye, another souvenir of World War II.

During an interview, when his ears are cocked to catch the questions, he points the right ear at you—the left ear went dead on him in North Africa.

Only a war could inflict casualties on Jack Ford—he proved too durable for the normal ravages of Hollywood. "Yes, I have had the same cook for sixteen years, the same pair of house slippers for twenty-eight, the same wife for thirty-two, the same house for thirty-one—it's only my bottle of gin that I have replaced every other evening!"

We stopped taking notes on the last part of that quote, Ford laughed.

"It's perfectly all right to print that—my friends know I have been on the wagon since '40."

Prior to that, his evenings were sometimes legendary. Not a man to knuckle under to convention, Ford never managed to be present at the Academy Award dinners at which he was awarded Oscars—three of them.

From the *New York Herald Tribune,* August 17, 1952. 1+. © 1952 by the *New York Times.* Reprinted by permission.

"What happened? Simple. Once I went fishing. Another time there was a war on . . . and on another occasion, I remember, I was suddenly taken *drunk!"*

Ford's early days in Hollywood conditioned him for combat. He followed his older brother, Francis, who was a director and, as Frank Ford, a male serial star. Frank put Jack to work as a prop boy in cliff-hangers, but when stunt men balked at some of the rough stuff the script called for, Frank shamed them by yelling:

"You call that dangerous! Why my kid brother could do it!"

To prove how safe it was, Jack was blown out of a tent, crashed a car after it was blasted by a land mine planted by Brother Frank, dived six stories from a freight car into a lake, etc. The only time a stunt sent Jack to the hospital was during the filming of a Civil War sequence, in which he doubled for the leading man. Frank set his camera for a closeup, and lobbed a smoke-bomb right under Jack's feet—a real Purple Heart!

Nineteen years later, Jack got even. Frank was cast in a John Ford movie this time, wearing a uniform and whiskers of a Confederate soldier, sitting on a wheelbarrow on the porch of a general store, chewing tobacco and spitting into the dusty street. Slyly, Jack had the wheelbarrow hitched to the axle of the buckboard in which the heroine was to make an escape from the villain. Jack still cherishes the memory of his brother's green face—"he swallowed the tobacco plug"—as the heroine whipped her horses down the street, with Brother Frank hanging onto the wheelbarrow in a swirl of dust and gravel.

"The score was finally even!"

The John Ford "stock company" of stars includes many famous, weather-beaten faces—Victor McLaglen, Thomas Mitchell, Barry Fitzgerald, Ward Bond—and the most famous of them now is a one-time prop boy who followed Ford's pattern in Chapter One of his career.

"I had to shoot the escape of two sailors from a submarine. It was a raging sea, and my two so-called stunt men said the trick was much too dangerous and wouldn't touch it. A sixty-four-year-old Irishman volunteered to try it, and I looked around for a husky partner. I spotted a big guy who worked in props, and I yelled at him, 'Hey, Duke, get in there!' Without hesitating, he shucked off his clothes, made a clean dive off the side of the tanker we used for a camera ship and played the scene with all the confidence of a swimmer who thinks he can stretch out and touch bottom. I took a good look at him and decided he was quite a boy—or quite a man—and pretty soon he was coming along so fast as an actor, we decided it was time for him to have a professional name. That's when we traded in 'Duke Morrison' for 'John Wayne.' "

Ford took his whole "stock company" to Ireland to shoot *The Quiet Man,* but the strangest assignment he ever gave them was to play "pitchmen" for Senator Taft, on television and in Chicago.

"Of course I worked to get the nomination for Taft, but I never could have voted for him. My father, bless him, would have sent me a sudden, swift message all the way from Heaven if he learned I had deserted the Democrats!"

John Ford Accords an Exclusive Interview to *Cinémonde*

JEAN MITRY/1955

THAT MORNING, JOHN FORD, still in bed, nevertheless invited me to come upstairs, granting *Cinémonde* the benefit of a private interview. His wife, while showing me into the luxurious apartment that the family occupies in the Royal Monceau, apologizes for her morning attire.

Mrs. Ford: "We were out very late last night. Paris is so marvelous and there is so much to see!"

But a gruff voice thunders from the other room.

Ford: "Come in! We are all in the family here, come in! It doesn't matter!"

Square-shouldered, stocky, youthfully sporting his sixty years, John Ford is finishing up taking in the morning news. An enormous cigar serves as an appetizer while breakfast is being prepared in the next room.

Ford: "Take one, will you?"

He holds out the box of cigars and I abandon my Gauloise for a comfortable Henry Clay. But here comes a young woman in a bathrobe and babouches. Then it's a tall guy's turn, very "leading man," who follows her in the same attire.

Ford: "My daughter Barbara. Mon gendre. C'est bien 'gendre,' n'est-ce-pas? Je parle si peu français oui, oui. . . ." ("My son-in-law. It's 'gendre' isn't it? I speaks so little French, yes, yes. . . .")

We exchange a few words, half-French, half-English with Ken Curtis and his ravishing wife, who presses her father to get up. Breakfast is ready.

From *Cinémonde,* January 14–20, 1955. Reprinted by permission of Janine Mitry. Translated from French by Jenny Lefcourt.

Ford: "Ok, ok, I'm coming! I came on a trip to Europe to rest and show my wife and my children Paris. It's the first time that they have crossed the ocean! We just spent a few days in Rome, and we are leaving the day after tomorrow for London. I don't have a minute to myself! Montmartre, Montparnasse, the Louvre, Notre-Dame, Versailles. These kids want to see everything."

Barbara: "And we won't see everything!" (Barbara excuses herself to go get dressed.)

Then a third person in a bathrobe appears, corpulent, greying.

Ford: "My cousin, the English director Brian Desmond Hurst. We are going to make a film together in Ireland, a little production of our own, for the pleasure. Three Irish stories. He will make one, I will make the two others, unless we are three, I don't know yet. Ah! I have to get dressed. Barbara! No, she isn't here . . . Excuse me a minute. . . ."

Desmond Hurst and I go to chat in the room next door. Desmond tells me about Ford's personal life, for the benefit of readers of *Cinémonde*.

In 1920, Ford married Mary McBride Smith, with whom he had two children: a son, Patrick Roper Ford, a journalist and writer, born in 1921, and a daughter, Barbara Nugent Ford, born in 1922, married today to the actor Ken Curtis.

But here comes Mrs. Ford with coffee, followed by Barbara.

Mrs. Ford: "My husband just had a serious operation two months ago, he is still in convalescence and these trips are very tiring. Yesterday, we were in Bayeux. We went to put flowers on the tombs of some friends killed during the Normandy landing, and in the evening the children want to go see a show. John likes the music-hall. We will have to go to the Folies-Bergère, to the Casino de Paris. In the meantime, he has to go to Versailles later. The admiral also has his obligations. Serious things first, no?"

Barbara: "And besides that, we have to organize that press conference. We have so little time. And to think that my father is here to rest after his operation!"

Ford: "Yes, yes . . . (putting on his jacket and coming back among us) a serious operation. The gall-bladder . . . yes! (he bursts out laughing) That's the way it is. That's life!"

With his eye which he keeps bandaged since the unfortunate accident during the war, he looks like one of the pirates of Treasure Island. A gruff and good-natured pirate.

Ford: "*War and Peace?* No, I won't do *War and Peace.* I have seen and filmed enough battle scenes. And besides, I'm not Russian, to reconstruct the atmosphere as it should be. A cup of coffee?"

Alas! John Ford, wanting to serve me, doesn't see a pot of boiling water prepared for the tea, and inadvertently spills the whole thing on his ankle. Everyone rushes over. He is terribly burned and I'm afraid he will retain a stinging memory of my visit. But the old lion is stoic. He coats his leg with cold cream. Already he talks to me of a big western he will undertake as soon as he returns to America, with John Wayne in the leading role: *The Searchers.* Pioneers who went to look for a little girl lost and taken in by the Indians.

Ford: "A very simple story as I like them. A strange adventure in the setting of the Rocky Mountains. My favorite films? Bah! I don't know. You say I made good films, I'll take your word for it. I didn't know people were so interested in my work in France. I'm delighted all the same. Well! Let's say *The Long Voyage Home, Stagecoach, The Informer.* Also *The Sun Shines Bright* and my last, *The Long Gray Line.* I think it's one of the best. You'll see. *The Quiet Man?* Yes, of course, especially because of the Irish climate. I made it in my home, in my country. All the extras were friends of the family. We shot it among friends. That's how I like to work. I hate affectation. You do your job, that's all. Sometimes it's good, sometimes it's less good, sometimes it's a failure. It happens to everyone! That's it."

But they are already coming to get John Ford.

Ford: "We'll see each other tomorrow," he says, excusing himself. "I hope I don't spill the coffee!"

Rendezvous with John Ford

BERT MILLER/1955

(PARIS.) A TALL, CIGAR-SMOKING, energetic man with thin
white hair on his head. A very high forehead, distinct nose, and pretty big
ears, large black glasses, and a black ribbon bandage over his left eye. One
could say that he is reminiscent of an ancient combatant crusader, a pirate.
But any possible dread that his appearance may have aroused in the by-
stander is driven away by his smile; and when he starts to explain about his
left eye, then one is simply captivated.

"That's a souvenir from the war," John Ford says. "My eye was part of the
price I had to pay for fighting for freedom and peace. You become something
of a philosopher when you have taken part in a rough war and seen the
transcience of everything up close. But . . . you are glad every time you return
to Paris. At least it is like itself, in spite of changes of government, in spite of
raised prices, and a lot of misery. For instance, the other day I visited the
Folies-Bergère. The last time I was there was in 1918. But it was exactly as if
time had stood still. The same locales, the same show, almost the same audience."

What is the art of making good films?

"It's hard to give a universal formula. But today I think the most important thing is to be in command of the art of borrowing money. A director
who wants to work autonomously, independently, freely—and we Irish are
among the most freedom-loving people—nowadays needs to raise the neces-

From *Filmnyheter*, vol. 10, no. 6, April, 1955, 4–6. Translated from Swedish by Ludvig Hertzberg.

sary capital himself for his difficult films. I like to say something with my films. And I'm a stubborn man, who prefers to work in a manner that I think personally appropriate. That's exactly why . . . after Paris, I'm on my way to Dublin and London. And in London, I'll be having a few nice fights with some money men to try to get them to let my hands free for the next films.

"For instance, here on my bedside table I have a new book, *The Searchers,* which makes up the material for my new films. It's a Western but not just with 'bang-bang' and cowboys and stuff. No, it has fine character studies, real problems, and a marvelous main character, whom I'm thinking John Wayne could play."

. . . . The last completed movie of John Ford's is a story about West Point, the U.S. military academy, called *The Long Gray Line.*

"I have been accused of being interested in masculine subjects. War and prison life have fascinated me over the years. But is that so strange? I have lived through the experience of two world wars. I myself have experienced the hell that is war. But I have also learned about friendship, bravery, and deprivation. And back home in Ireland, I learned what a poor life means in a barren climate. And the sea, and the hardship of men at sea have fascinated me since early youth. Would I not then have betrayed my ideals, my thoughts, and my ancestors, if I hadn't given men like that a well-deserved celebration in my films? If I hadn't chosen to tell about poor, simple people and their hard struggle for existence?"

With that, John Ford lit a cigar.

Recalling a 1955 Interview with John Ford

GEORGE BLUESTONE/1955

A WALKING CYCLONE WITH a cyclone's energy, he came rolling into the offices of his producer, Merian C. Cooper, an hour late (I'd been warned about this), acting "John Ford" even before he'd negotiated the door. He was wearing a pink and black striped shirt, a safari hat, and thick glasses over the famous eye patch. "Son, my editor held me up," he said.

I was there to ask questions about Ford's adaptations of *The Informer* and *The Grapes of Wrath,* which I would be discussing in my book, *Novels into Film.* While waiting, I'd been thumbing through a stack of photographs from *The Searchers,* Ford's current project. I picked out a beautiful still of a lone Indian on a horse riding an immaculate dune. Ford removed his thick lens, held the photo about three inches from his good eye, and made an approving grunt. "Yeah, it is pretty, isn't it?"

He positioned himself in a chair, ready to begin. Cooper, sunburned, bald and dapper, had been wandering in and out of the office. Ford gave the legendary co-director of *King Kong* a look, which signaled him to leave us alone. Cooper obligingly disappeared until our talk was over. I began by asking Ford questions I'd had about the production of *The Grapes of Wrath,* accumulated over months of research, including an interview with screenwriter Nunnally Johnson. Ford was almost dismissive of the film. "It was a work from my dark period," he said, treating it like an aberration of youth.

Soon it was clear that he wasn't going to give serious answers. "What happened to your Oakies after they settled in California?" I asked. He replied,

---

as if he'd given the same reply dozens of times. "They took over the State. One of them, a contractor, does something in the building trades—lives across the street from me. His home is a palace compared to mine!" And so it went. . . . We were half-way through out interview when Ford looked up at me as if we'd just now been introduced and said, "How about you? Where did you come from? Where are you going?"

I lapsed into a sketchy autobiography. My father was a Russian immigrant. I was raised on the East Side of New York. I'd attended Harvard on a scholarship, and I was currently at Johns Hopkins writing *Novels into Film* for my doctorate. Now Ford listened very attentively, as if he were trying to absorb the design of my life. He was nearly sixty when we spoke, and something had clicked on his radar screen. Was it the struggles of a twenty-seven-year-old kid to write one of the country's first Ph.D.'s about the movies?

In his own inimitable way, Ford was responding, I think, to the courtesy of being taken seriously. There were no books about his career at the time. I had, after all, made the pilgrimage to Los Angeles exclusively to see him. For a few tantalizing minutes, he had become the serious questioner himself, I the respondent. Ford picked up on something I'd said, that I'd gone to the Iowa Writers Workshop for my Master's. "Workshop? Workshop?" he asked. "Is that one of those pinko outfits?"

I began patiently to explain that "Workshop" wasn't a labor reference. It was normal usage for a group of writers getting together to read each other's work. Instructing the great man, I felt suddenly foolish. He knew perfectly well what a "Workshop" was. He was baiting me to see how I would react; the look in his good eye was marvellous, half mischievous, half mocking. If he was impelled to test the youngster from Hopkins, what must life have been like, I wondered, for poor actors when Ford was the director in charge? Like so many legends about Ford, everything was double—at least. Curmudgeon and teddy bear. Good-natured ribbing and aggressive baiting.

Before I left with a handful of notes, Ford picked up the still I admired from *The Searchers,* took out a green felt pen and inscribed it: "To George Bluestone with affectionate thanks, Jack Ford." (The photograph sat on my mantlepiece for nine years, until it disappeared at a time I moved to London to work in film production.)

I thought my contact with Ford had ended with that interview. But there was an epilogue. When *Novels into Film* was published in 1957, I sent Ford a copy, but got no acknowledgement. In 1960, teaching at the University of

Washington in Seattle, I arranged what was perhaps the first John Ford retrospective, concentrating on the rich middle years from *Stagecoach* to *My Darling Clementine*. Again, I sent Ford a program, expecting no reply. However, the day before the *Clementine* screening, and five years after our interview, I got a telephone call from the film's director. A local one. "Don't get the idea that I'm up here for the retrospective. I'm up here to get my associate's daughter into the University of Washington."

Without thinking, I gave him the name of a friend in the admissions office. "Well," I said, "as long as you're up here, how about introducing *My Darling Clementine*?" He agreed to be there. The following night, the house was packed, and Ford appeared on time, which I took as a sign from heaven. He was wearing a white turtleneck jersey with a teal blue suit. In his introductory remarks he related the old saw about how in the early days actors were pariahs. "They used to have signs in windows reading, 'Dogs and actors need not apply.' "

Unfortunately, he said nothing about *Clementine,* and that was it. After his introduction, he was going back to the hotel to have a steak dinner with his associate Max.

I stayed to see the film. It had been a while since I had screened it and I wanted to refresh my memory of the details. So I was a little surprised when the auditorium door opened, a few minutes into the picture, and I saw Ford finding a seat in the back. I went over and took the seat next to his. "What are you doing here?" I whispered.

"It's okay, they serve until ten," he whispered back. We sat through the film, and when the famous hoedown scene came on, with all its lyrical pleasure, Ford leaned over and said, "Hey, you know this isn't a bad movie. I haven't seen it in a while." I noticed he sat with his good eye favoring the screen.

Later we went to his room, where Max was waiting for him. Max was Ford's accountant. Though Max's participation was mostly monosyllabic, he seemed to have come up mainly to keep Ford company. However, he *had* talked to my friend in the admissions office. Ford never did order his steak, but he knocked back four bourbons as we talked far into the night. The late hour blurred my eventual memory, but I remember an extended anecdote involving John Wayne, a pit bull, and a homemade distillery. Another about an Irish nun on her first trip to New York. Above all, a story about some church bells in Dublin. "They were the purest, clearest, most beautiful sound in the world. I stood there, listening for an hour. I wish you could have heard it, Bloomstone."

"Bluestone," I corrected.

"Aren't you the one with the Russian immigrant parents?" Five years had gone by, and he remembered, sort of.

"My father was Russian. My mother was Rumanian. It's still Bluestone." But I was Bloomstone the rest of the night. I don't know how I eventually got home, but I drove all right, because the morning after my car was intact in the driveway. The last thing Ford said to me was, "Nice book." It took me a few beats to realize that he meant *Novels into Film*. He'd remembered that, too.

Poet in an Iron Mask

MICHAEL KILLANIN/1958

AMONG THE CINEMA'S FEW POETS, director John Ford is a
man of iron will. Combined with his good humor is a determination to make
the film . . . his way. This article is a new evaluation of Ford's contribution to
cinema by a man who knows him well. They worked together when Ford
went to Ireland to make *The Quiet Man*; and Lord Killanin was producer on
both *The Rising of the Moon* and *Gideon's Day*.

"... I have known John Ford all my life. Strange as it may seem, I have
learnt more about the substance of his genius during the making of *Gideon's
Day* in Britain than during the making of any of his other films. Much of the
understanding comes from the day to day arguments and discussions between shots, such as the following which I thought worth recording."

KILLANIN: *Jack, now that we have been associated with three pictures, what
do you think really rules your choice in making a film—characterization, story
value, or the setting and location?*
FORD: Surely you know by now that the most difficult to find is the story.
Once we have found the right story, it is the responsibility of the writer,
director, and producer to work as a team to put it on paper in such a way
that it can be a guide to what we have to put on the screen.

KILLANIN: *I certainly know that once you are on the floor it is a matter for the
director and the cameraman to produce the eventual product which is seen on the
screen.*

From *Films and Filming*, vol. 4, no. 5. February 1958. 9, 28.

FORD: I have made 118 pictures: and what surprises me working in England is how little cutting is done in the camera. Perhaps I have learned from experience of bad cutters not to give them anything with which to make a mess!

Everything I shoot is cut in the camera and I do not cover myself from every angle, which appears to be the desire of some of the front-office English executives.

KILLANIN: *We seem to be spending a lot of time on casting. Whilst I may have had predetermined views on casting, you more often than not suggest types quite different to that indicated in the script.*
FORD: But don't you see, I am interested in *people*. That is why in a picture like *Gideon's Day* and, indeed, *The Rising of the Moon* where we had some fifty speaking characters, all the parts "sing." I certainly don't like type casting. I like casting for individuals, for I photograph people.

KILLANIN: *One of the troubles I have always had as a producer is that actors are always trying to sneak in to see rushes. Thank goodness you've stopped all that.*
FORD: Well Michael, you know I do not believe in actors seeing rushes. It is only the director who knows what he is trying to get and who is composing the whole. If the actor sees his rushes one day, he may try to change his personality the next day and make it more difficult for me in the process.

KILLANIN: *Yes, watching you direct is like watching the conductor on the rostrum before a symphony orchestra. On both* The Rising of the Moon *where we had Frank Nugent as script writer, and* Gideon's Day *where we had T. E. B. Clarke, the eventual pictures have gone a long way from the shooting script.*
FORD: Because as the basic story develops one must develop each character in the actor, besides the mood and the tempo, so that the drama is correctly mixed with humour.

KILLANIN: *Certainly many actors and actresses have found their first opportunity in your pictures. On the other hand, there are always a number of actors who will appear time and again in one of your productions.*
FORD: Well, it's natural to use people whose capabilities one knows and also they know my method of work. It has certainly been an interesting experience during the last two years working both in Ireland and England where there is such tremendous talent among actors. Jack Hawkins, for instance,

who plays a Police Inspector in *Gideon's Day* is, I believe, the finest dramatic actor with whom I have worked.

KILLANIN: *But reverting to stories. With our Irish company, Four Provinces Films, I am continually reading and considering stories which might be made in Ireland, not necessarily Irish subjects. One of our troubles is that Irish stories are always more literary than dramatic. There is one hand pulling us towards the making of good but cheap pictures for TV and the other trying to make feature pictures of quality. What should we do in the future?*

FORD: Well Michael, you know any picture I make is only making money for the tax collectors. I took no salary for either *Gideon's Day* or *The Rising of the Moon*; but I have rarely made a film where I did not like the story. As for TV, I think it has interesting possibilities for the future and let's face it, *The Rising of the Moon* was shot in such a way that it could be used as three TV stories. In the long run the length or time of a picture depends on the story. Let's find the right stories to make, then decide their scale and market potential!

Down with Rebecca

N E W S W E E K / 1 9 5 8

ONE OF THE TRUE anomalies in Hollywood is director John Ford, who has won six Oscars even though he has always said exactly what he pleased. Talking to a visitor last week about the forthcoming *The Last Hurrah,* which he had just finished making for Columbia, Ford was exhilaratingly exact as ever.

"I had hoped to make a controversial picture," said Ford. "That was originally Harry Cohn's idea [as studio chief of Columbia]. He wanted it controversial, exactly like the book. Then, after we had been only three or four days on it, Cohn died. The new men—seven or eight of them—thought it was just too daring. 'It's liable to offend people,' they said. Well, you can't keep doing *Rebecca of Sunnybrook Farm.* Anyway, the moles—a whole series of them— have been working on it. But there's still lots of good stuff left in. There is practically no love story, and no sex. Yet I think it makes you gulp in a couple of places."

James Michael Curley, eighty-three-year-old ex-mayor of Boston and ex-governor of Massachusetts, whom most people took to be the political boss portrayed in the novel the movie was made from, has lately tried to stop Columbia from showing the film on the ground that it violated property rights to his own autobiography and constitutes an invasion of privacy.

"It's certainly not James Michael Curley's life," said Ford. "It has nothing to do with it. But I'll say this to Curley: If this is Curley—if Curley thinks he is Frank Skeffington—then instead of suing I would advise him to run for governor again."

The Skeffington of the story is the classical political boss, "handsome, white-haired, bright of eye, ruddy of face—and a year either side of sixty." Ford waited a whole year and went without salary during that time to get Spencer Tracy for the part. "He's perfect," said Ford. "His body, for one thing, is just right—a big old man's body, yet it's up and alive when people are about. Every little thing about this man's character is in Tracy's portrayal. I think he's just great."

The picture as a whole, though, had a narrow escape. "The moles got the great idea of cutting out one and a half reels. Everybody had to get in on the act and save the picture. In the end we put back two reels, and it comes out the way I made it. I'm stubborn, too."

This stubbornness has been operating ever since Ford, now sixty-three, went to Hollywood from Maine in 1915 (the year of D. W. Griffith's *Birth of a Nation*). Ford started work as a property boy, became a stunt man, an actor, an assistant director, and finally, at twenty, a full director (at $35 a week). The movies he has made since then have included *Stagecoach, The Informer, How Green Was My Valley, Grapes of Wrath,* and *The Quiet Man.* He has made some 320 [sic] films, but the only picture he has liked so far, he says ("the only one to come off as I had hoped") is *The Fugitive,* a movie he made in 1947 about religious persecution in Mexico, and a box-office failure.

Probably his most frequently praised movie is his twenty-three-year-old *The Informer,* which figures large in all the movie histories. "I never cared for *The Informer,*" Ford said. "I still occasionally see it, and still wonder what the hell all the shouting is about. It's pretty obvious."

Ford, a gruff, loquacious man with a dry wit and a sharp tongue, has some-times been accused of projecting his real but hidden sentimentalism into his pictures. "A made-up statement," he says. "I'm sentimental as hell. I'm Irish. I like animals, and then, after baseball, I like people."

He has little taste for the way movies are made today. "In the old days, you turned them out and got the cost back. Now it's a carefully calculated risk, and the director doesn't have much to say about it, either. There was a time when a director could pick his own stories. Now the producers read stories in their advance proofs, nail the property down, and the poor director takes what he's given."

Ford is a difficult man to handle; as one man has put it: "You don't handle

Ford; you turn the reins loose and you try to hang on." He stays aloof from organized Hollywood social life, shuns previews and night clubs, spends much of his time on his yacht, *Aramer,* which he keeps in Honolulu.

The picture he is tackling next is *The Horse Soldiers*—"all about Grierson's raid. He raised hell and managed to get away with it in the Confederate country between La Grange, Tenn., and Baton Rouge. It's a pretty good horse yarn.

"The first 'motion' pictures were Leland Stanford's photos of a running horse. For your information, a running horse remains the finest subject for a motion-picture camera." There will be plenty of horses in the new movie.

A Meeting with John Ford

JEAN-LOUIS RIEUPEYROUT/1961

TWO STEPS OFF SUNSET Strip—the section of Sunset Strip which is home to the most famous nightclubs of Hollywood—is the little house on Palm Avenue where John Ford's office can be found. The house is comfortable and cool (air condition is incontestably the number one invention of this country). On the walls, watercolor portraits of Tom Mix, Harry Carey, Buck Jones. John Wayne in his uniform of *Fort Apache* is painted in oil. In this very western environment, the master of the house welcomes me, kindly, like a grandfather receiving a visitor, and invites me to take a seat.

Ford—I was in France, but I forgot almost all my French, excuse me. At the end of the War, I was at the Mont Saint-Michel. Decorated, embraced by a French general with a beard. Wounded too. . . . I am a little deaf. . . . I am of Irish origin, but of western culture, Yankee. . . . In Europe, everyone hates the Yankees. Can you cite one European who is pro-American? . . .

I am a liberal, not a Communist; people think I'm a racist, but in Arizona, in New Mexico, many Southerners have settled, and it is not surprising that in my films these characters have racist sentiments. In the East, they think that what I show is false, but . . . that's the way it was. What interests me is the folklore of the West. To show the real, almost documentary. . . . I was a cowboy; I earned $13 a month with my hands, not bad, huh? At the time when Pancho Villa crossed the border. . . . I like fresh air, wide open spaces,

From *Cinema 61*, no. 53. February 1961. 8–10. Reprinted by permission of the author. Translated from French by Jenny Lefcourt.

the mountains, the deserts. . . . Sex, obscenity, degeneracy, these things don't interest me. . . .

Wagon Master? You didn't see it in France? Why? It's the best, you know. No great actors, no pistol shots, but real men. The picture didn't make much money. In England, they project it and discuss it. I talked about it at Oxford and Cambridge, at conferences.

Yes, I receive a lot of screenplays. . . . My next film? I forgot the title. Big actors, but the story is worthless. It's for the money. . . . You understand? It pays. . . . Money!''

Three quarters of an hour have gone by in galloping conversation. One remark must be made: Ford is not a man to dwell upon his work at length. He says, and insists, ''That's the way it was.''

The Old Wrangler Rides Again

BILL LIBBY / 1964

NOT UNLIKE A PERSON from another place and another time, a displaced character out of his beloved Old West, director John Ford swept from the sun-baked streets of Sunset Boulevard into his small, plush Hollywood offices. He was a picture of khakied inelegance, preceded by two wildly barking dachshunds. One of the office girls rushed to corral the dogs; the others pressed their backbones to the wall to clear a path for the briskly striding figure.

Ford settled into a chair behind his desk, cupped his hands, and a secretary rushed to shove a huge, steaming mug of coffee into them. He swallowed from his cup, flipped a match on a rug, and turned to me: "I've been damned as a 'Western director,' " he said. "Every time I start to make a Western, they say: 'There goes senile old John Ford out West again,' but I don't give a damn. I've done a lot of pictures in my lifetime that weren't Westerns, but I've also done a lot that were, and I'm going to do a lot more. I don't think they need any defense at all."

Ford is not an easy man to see. He says he can count on the fingers of one hand the full interviews he's granted in the last ten years. He succumbed to me simply because I held out as lure this defense of his favorite topic. "You're supposed to be an illiterate if you like Westerns," he growled. "What nonsense! Is it more intelligent to prefer pictures about sex and crime, sex maniacs, prostitutes, and narcotics addicts? Is it more intelligent to prefer a picture simply because it's a foreign film and has subtitles? It may be more

From *Cosmopolitan*, vol. 156, no. 3. March 1964. 12–21.

fashionable, but it isn't more intelligent. I'm not a vain man. I don't like talking about my own work. But it's time those of us who make Westerns, or go to them, or enjoy them in any way, stopped ducking into dark alleys when the subject is brought up. It's time we spoke up."

Speak up he did, drinking one hot mug of coffee after another, chain-smoking cigars and tossing the butts roughly and often inaccurately in the direction of an ash tray a little smaller than the Grand Canyon.

It is easy to be fooled by such a man. His outer senses are dulled and he is no longer young. He has been making movies forever. When you ask him a question, you must wait against a long silence for a reply, until you begin to wonder if he has forgotten or even heard you in the first place. But when he has considered your question carefully, he will give you your answer, and if it has been a foolish question, his answer will mock you and make you seem a fool, and if it has been a good question, his answer will be good and make you feel good.

"When a motion picture is at its best," he said, "it is long on action and short on dialogue. When it tells its story and reveals its characters in a series of simple, beautiful, active pictures, and does it with as little talk as possible, then the motion picture medium is being used to its fullest advantage. I don't know any subject on earth better suited to such a presentation than a Western.

"The people who coined that awful term 'horse opera' are snobs. The critics are snobs. Now, I'm not one who hates all critics. There are many good ones and I pay attention to them and I've even acted on some of their suggestions. But most criticism has been destructive, full of inaccuracies, and generalizations. Hell, I don't think the leading newspaper reviewers even go to see most of the Westerns. They send their second string assistants. And they're supposed to be very nasty and very funny in their reviews. Well, it's a shame, because it makes it a crime to like a Western. Sure, there have been bad and dishonest Westerns. But, there have been bad and dishonest romantic stories, too, and war stories, and people don't attack all romantic movies or war movies because of these. Each picture should be judged on its own merit. In general, Westerns have maintained as high a level as that of any other theme.

"The critics always say we make Westerns because it's an easy way to make money. This is hogwash. They're not cheap or easy to make. They have to be done on location, which is damned hard work, the most expensive and most difficult form of moviemaking. It's true Westerns generally make money.

What the hell's wrong with that? They make money because people like them. And what the hell's wrong with that? If there was more concern with what the public wants and less with what the critics want, Hollywood wouldn't be in the awful fix it's in right now. This is a business. If we can give the public what it wants, then it's a good business and makes money. The audience is happy and we're happy. What the hell's wrong with that?

"Some of our greatest Americans have been Western fans. I guess in many cases it provided them with an escape, a relief, but I see nothing wrong with that. Woodrow Wilson, Franklin Roosevelt, Jack Kennedy were all Western fans.

"Yes, that's right, they were all Democrats, and I'm a Democrat, too. I don't try to hide that, either. But some Republicans have been great Western fans—Douglas MacArthur. I flew from Korea into Tokyo once, years ago, and MacArthur sent for me. He said they were showing movies that night and that the picture was one of mine, *She Wore a Yellow Ribbon.* He said he was showing it in my honor, that he watched it at least once a month and never got tired of seeing it. Now that *is* an honor."

I asked Ford who attends Westerns. "Everyone," he said brusquely. Then he smiled. "Actually, we've taken surveys and we've found that most of our audience is made up of children and fathers taking their children. The fathers enjoy Westerns and the children give them an excuse to go. It's a shame that most persons feel they have to sneak in to see a Western by the side door. There's nothing wrong with anything being 'family entertainment,' you know. But now Hollywood has found it can pull a lot of people to the box office and make a lot of money with a lot of different types of pictures. Lately, they've been doing it with 'dirty pictures.' I don't like to use that term, but I don't know what else you can call them.

"Now, I'm a Roman Catholic. But, I'm Irish, too. I think I'm fairly masculine and I don't think I'm a prude, but I do think there are certain things that don't belong on the screen. I wouldn't take anyone to see some of the pictures that are being put out today. I wouldn't even take them to see the billboards outside of the movie houses. These and other ads, lurid come-ons with half-naked women, are dishonest and cater to our worst instincts. They aren't making Hollywood any friends.

"When I come back from making a Western on location, I feel a better man for it. I don't think some of the modern trash makes anyone feel better for having read or seen it.

"I don't recall a Western which ever had to carry a 'For Adults Only' sign. When you go to a movie today, you feel guilty, as though you were going to a striptease. It all runs in cycles. Tomorrow, someone will make a picture about a boy and a dog and it'll make money and then everyone will start making boy-and-dog pictures again.

"Actually, I'm certainly not against sex on the screen if it's done in the right way. Many Westerns have a gusty sort of sex. And I think I made the sexiest picture ever, *The Quiet Man*. Now this was all about a man trying to get a woman into bed, but that was all right, they were married, and it was essentially a moral situation, done with honesty, good taste, and humor. These things are all fundamental to a good Western, too. In a Western, you can make a strong picture which is reasonably adult, yet a man can still take his children to see it, which is the way it should be. After all, we're not in the burlesque business.

"I know the term 'morality play' has been applied to Westerns, but I won't go that far, nor be so high-toned about it, but I do feel they have a basically moral quality, and I applaud this and think it's the way it should be.

"We use immoral characters. In *Stagecoach,* we had Claire Trevor playing a woman of easy virtue and Thomas Mitchell playing a drunken doctor. We don't deny that there are such persons; we just aren't out to glorify them or build every story around them. Incidentally, these have become stock characters in Westerns and maybe they've become what you call 'clichés,' but they weren't always clichés, and I keep trying to do things fresh or different, just as many others in this business do.

"There are no more clichés in Westerns than in anything else, and this applies to our moral approach, too. I don't think I, nor anyone else, have always garbed my heroes in white and my villains in black and so forth. Good doesn't always triumph over evil. It doesn't in life and it doesn't in all Westerns. Usually it does, but I think this is the way it should be. I have depicted some sad and tragic and unjust things in my Westerns, as have others.

"I remember once I was seated in a screening room with someone viewing the rushes of a picture I was shooting. In an early scene, there was a background shot of a man on a horse. It was background, mind you; he wasn't important and the scene wasn't. This person turned to me and said he knew that was the villain. He was wearing black or riding a black horse or some such fool thing. I threw him the hell out. I had to cut the scene out. It's not fair. It's one of those unfair generalizations made about Westerns."

What, I wondered, were the men of the West really like?

"They were like Will Rogers," Ford said, waving at the wall. He stood staring at a blank spot on the wall. He buzzed his secretary and she came rushing in, thrusting another steaming mug of coffee into his hands and turning to run. He pinned her to the door with a shout: "Where the hell is my Will Rogers picture? When am I going to get it back? When I loaned it out, they promised to return it. Would you be kind and generous enough to get those kind and generous people on the phone and ask them when can I kindly have my Will Rogers picture back?"

"Yes, Sir, Mr. Ford," she shouted back. "Right away, Sir."

When she had made her escape, he looked down to find coffee in his hands, and raised the cup to his lips. He flipped a cigar butt away, missing the Grand Canyon, lit another, puffed it, and stared at the wall. "I had a picture of Will Rogers and, by God, I'll get it back," he said. He turned to me. "The men of the West were like Will Rogers. They were rugged and imperfect men, but many were basically gentle, and most were basically moral and religious, like most people who live with the land.

"They had their own language, but it was not profane. They had a warm, rugged, natural good humor. Strong people have always been able to laugh at their own hardships and discomforts. Soldiers do in wartime. The old cowboy did in the Old West. And today, in the hinterlands, in places like Montana and Wyoming, there are working cowboys, and they even carry guns, usually .30-.30 Winchesters, though for protection against animals, such as coyotes, not to shoot each other.

"We've studied the history of these cowboys, past and present, and we've had some true Western characters, such as Pardner Jones, serving as technical experts on our films. I think some of the personality things I've mentioned have been very well portrayed in our Western film heroes. These men are natural. They are themselves. They are rugged individualists. They live an outdoor life, and they don't have to *conform*.

"I think one of the great attractions of the Western is that people like to identify themselves with these cowboys. We all have an escape complex. We all want to leave the troubles of our civilized world behind us. We envy those who can live the most natural way of life, with nature, bravely and simply. What was that character's name? Mitty, that's it. We're all Walter Mittys. We all picture ourselves doing heroic things. And there are worse heroes than the Westerners for us to have.

"The Western heroes may be 'larger than life,' but so are many of our historical heroes, and we hate to dispel the public's illusions. If we cast handsome men and attractive women in semibiographical roles, portraying persons who were really homely, we are doing no worse than has always been done in movies. I myself am a pretty ugly fellow. The public wouldn't pay to see me on film.

"It is probable that the Westerns have been most inaccurate in overglamorizing and overdramatizing the heroes and villains of the period, and in playing up the gunfights. We could do without such stock characters as the hero who leaps from two stories onto his horse, fires twenty shots at a time from his six-shooter and has a comical, bearded rascal for his sidekick. But again, these are generalizations, which don't apply to all Westerns.

"We have been charged with using too much violence, with too often achieving a good end through the unfortunate use of violent means, and this charge has merit, but, after all, those *were* violent times. I've tried not to overdo this and so have a lot of men who have turned out good Westerns. The very term 'gunslinger' makes us cringe, and we try to hold shoot-downs to a minimum. But men did carry guns and did shoot at each other. There wasn't much law for a long while, after all.

"It is wrong to make heroic the villainous characters, such as Billy the Kid, who were more ruthless and vicious than anyone can imagine today. However, it is true that much of the conversion to law and order was accomplished by reformed criminals, who got sheriffs' jobs because of their strong reputations. Men like Wyatt Earp had real nerve. They didn't have to use their guns. They overpowered the opposition with their reputations and personalities. They faced them down. They were lucky. A .45 is the most inaccurate gun ever made. If you've handled one, you know. Pardner Jones told me if you put Wild Bill Hickok in a barn with a six-shooter, he couldn't have hit the wall.

"It is equally wrong for the heroes to have been made out to be pure Sir Galahads in so many cases, which is nonsense. However, those were different times than we know today. Mere survival took something a little out of the ordinary, and the men who dominated the time *were* out of the ordinary, really big men.

"Some of the early Western stars, such as William S. Hart and Buck Jones, were real Western types, either from the West or naturals for the part. They were great and courageous athletes and horsemen, skills which deserve some credit. Tom Mix was a great athlete and, I think, next to C. B. De Mille, our greatest showman. I worked often and happily with George O'Brien, a fine Western actor. And also Harry Carey, through whom we brought the real saddle tramp to the screen for the first time. He was natural and rugged, but he had an innate modesty. He was a great, great actor, maybe the best Westerner ever. Will Rogers was a real Westerner, a truly outstanding character actor, humorist, and person, who did much to popularize the real cowboy. I used to have a fine picture of him up there on the wall and I intend to get it back.

"Because the roles such actors played were natural roles and because they played them naturally and simply, they have never been given enough credit for their acting skills. Even those that date back to the silents seem less exaggerated, more natural to us than the romantic heroes of that period, as we see these early films once again. But the critics seem to think you have to be conscious of acting for it to be acting. Actually, the less conscious you are that it is acting, the better it usually is.

"There have been many fine Western actors in recent years damned with this casual acceptance. Henry Fonda has been one. Gary Cooper was another. Coop even came not to believe in himself. But if Coop said he wasn't a great actor, he was wrong. And he *was* a real Westerner. He was just as fine in *High Noon* as he was in *Sergeant York,* and I'm glad the critics saw fit to reward him equally for both.

"Many of our fine Western actors, such as Jimmy Stewart, who is terrific, have had to go outside Westerns to get their rewards. Two who have never received anywhere near the credit they deserve are two of my closest friends and men with whom I've made many films, John Wayne and Ward Bond.

"Wayne is one of our most popular actors and a great box office draw, something which should not be disregarded. And he is superb. As long ago as *The Long Voyage Home,* he proved he was a fine actor. When I made *She Wore a Yellow Ribbon,* we had Wayne playing an old man. The critics announced in advance Wayne wasn't capable of playing an old man. Then they didn't bother to judge for themselves. But he did it, and beautifully. It was a very moving performance.

"I miss old Ward Bond very much. He played *Wagon Master* for me in the early days, and it's possible his very successful TV *Wagon Train* role was modeled after this. He was a great human being and a wonderful actor who was taken for granted because he played Westerns.

"It has been said that we haven't always portrayed women fairly in Westerns, and I think there's some truth in that, though not a great deal. It is a sort of a sore spot. The men were dominant in settling the West. The women played a somewhat lesser role, though certainly an important one. There were the saloon women. There always will be wherever there are rugged and lonely men. And some of these were not such terrible characters. And there were the home women who helped break the land, bear and raise children and make a home for their families. These were hard times for women and they acquitted themselves nobly. And I think they've generally been portrayed very well by actresses. Claire Trevor is one example. Jane Darwell, a grand person and a grand actress, is another."

Ford has won six Oscars, two for wartime documentaries, and four for feature films. He was honored for *The Informer* in 1935; *The Grapes of Wrath* in 1940; *How Green Was My Valley* in 1941; and *The Quiet Man* in 1952. But he has never been honored as director for any of his great Westerns.

"It is hard for me to judge," he says, "but I would say *Stagecoach, She Wore a Yellow Ribbon,* and *The Searchers* were my best Westerns. I also remember *The Iron Horse* and *Wagon Master* fondly. And I think some of my more recent ones, such as *The Man Who Shot Liberty Valance,* stand up very well, too. I like to think *Stagecoach* set a trend, sort of blazed a trail, for the adult western, and it *is* appreciated, but it did not win me an Oscar. I don't like to say 'I'm proud' of the pictures that did win, but I do remember them fondly. Still, I'll be darned if I worked any less seriously on some of my Westerns, and I think they're just as good."

He pointed out that of the pictures that brought him Oscars for the best direction, only *How Green Was My Valley* was also selected as the best picture. And he threw in the names of some of his other pictures that didn't win him Oscars but which he felt were just as good as those that did: *The Long Voyage Home; Young Mr. Lincoln;* Irvin Cobb's *The Sun Shines Bright;* and *When Willie Comes Marching Home* with Dan Dailey, which he considers "the funniest film ever made." He also noted that some great Westerns made by other men also lost out in the quest for Hollywood's major awards. These include *The Ox-Bow Incident, Shane,* and *Red River.*

"Oscars aren't the end-all of our business," he growled nastily. "The award those of us in this profession treasure most highly is the New York Film Critics Award. And those of us in the directing end treasure the Directors Guild of America Award. These are eminently fair."

Yet it is a fact that even these have been snobbish about Westerns. *High Noon,* and its director, Fred Zinnemann, did win the New York Film Critics Awards. Ford won it four times, for *The Informer; Stagecoach; The Grapes of Wrath* and *The Long Voyage Home* (in the same year); and *How Green Was My Valley.* Miss Kerr did win this prize for her woman of the soil in *The Sundowners.* George Stevens won the Directors Guild Award for *Giant* (also *A Place in the Sun*), while Ford won it for *The Quiet Man,* but never for a Western.

"Well, the applause of the critics isn't the end-all of our business, either," Ford said, his voice cracking with contempt. "But when awards and such things influence public opinion, it's damned unfortunate. Do you think I let Oscars influence me? What is the Academy Award anyway? Who is a member? Who votes? I'm not a member. Do you know that only a couple of hundred people vote each year? Is that supposed to represent all of us? None of us really give a good damn about the Academy. I've never even been to one of their shindigs, not even to receive one of my awards."

He stared reflectively into his mug of coffee. His voice mellowed for a moment. "Oh, I'm pleased when I'm honored," he said. "I'm just not fooled by it. I don't think it's the measure of my success. I don't think John Wayne thinks his lack of awards is the measure of his success. I hope not. I love that damn Republican," he grinned.

He pointed to some pictures of Indians on the wall, and had me look at them. "The Indian is very close to my heart," he said. He had a deer hide inscribed to him with affection from the Navajo, and he asked me to pick it up and feel it and read the gracious inscription.

"There's some merit to the charge that the Indian hasn't been portrayed accurately or fairly in the Western, but again, this charge has been a broad generalization and often unfair. The Indian didn't welcome the white man, you know, and he wasn't diplomatic. We were enemies and we fought. The fight against the Indian was fundamental to the story of the West. If he has been treated unfairly by the whites in films, that, unfortunately, was often the case in real life. There was much racial prejudice in the West. Some of it was directed against the Negro, too, by the way, something I touched on in *Sergeant Rutledge.*

"The Indians are wonderful people. I have come to know best the Navajo of Monument Valley. The Navajo can ride like a son of a gun and they're the greatest damn fighters in the world. They were tough to beat in the Old West and they've been tough to beat in modern war, in which many of them fought for us and performed heroically. But even today, although the Indian has a better civilized understanding of us, we don't have a much better understanding of him. There's still a lot of prejudice.

"When we first went into the Indians' reservations, they were poor and starving. The pay from the shooting of *Stagecoach* helped put them on their feet. Since then, many movies on location have helped and rewarded the Indian. I don't mean we should take too much credit for this, or that it makes up for our treatment of them on film, but it is a fact, and it's been important to them. Many of the Indians are wealthy now, through the discovery of oil on their property, but except for a few luxuries, they actually still live as they always have, simply and close to the land. They're not greatly different than they were, particularly not at heart.

"I am doing now a particular story I've wanted to do which stresses the Indian angle. It's called *Cheyenne Autumn*. It won't be the first film to deal sympathetically with them. Since the early years, a lot of movie-makers have tried to see at least some of the Indian side of the problem. Television hasn't dealt too much with the Indian, but has concentrated more on the whites in the Old West. Under the handicaps it faces, TV has done a wonderful job with Westerns in general.

"However, when you get down to this matter of treating various phases of the Old West inaccurately, TV has been a worse offender than the movies. More than the movies, TV has glamorized and dramatized their heroes inaccurately. And many of the TV Westerns are just plain bad, just like many of the movie Westerns. I don't sympathize with anyone who sits glued to his set for hours on end, watching any of this that comes along. In this respect, I guess it's just as well my eyesight prevents me watching more.

"But in general, I don't think there is any aspect of our history that has been as well or completely portrayed on the screen, particularly in movies, as the Old West.

"Ambitious projects along this line are constantly coming along. One of the latest is *How the West Was Won,* which was done in separate segments. I was one of the directors on one section, a very short piece of material in which a boy returns to the farm from the Civil War, then leaves to head West. I have seen it on the screen and was pleased to find it touching and strong. And it is more or less a very true situation.

"There have to be some compromises with historical fact and accuracy in all movies. The public will simply not accept certain things which seem strange to them, true as they may be. You cannot, for example, show a general heading into battle, riding a mule, wearing corduroys and a pith helmet, and shielding himself from the sun with an umbrella, yet General Crook actually did that.

"Most Westerners really dressed in simple, rugged clothing, and were often very dirty. You got dirty on the range, you know, and laundries and bathrooms were sometimes hard to come by. Some time ago we reached the point where they would let our characters get out of the elaborate dress that once passed in movies for cowboy clothes, and let us put John Wayne, for example, into a part without a coat and with suspenders showing, as in *The Horse Soldiers*.

"Actually, the thing most accurately portrayed in the Western is the land. I think you can say that the real star of my Westerns has always been the land. I have always taken pride in the photography of my films, and the photography of Westerns in general has often been outstanding, yet rarely draws credit. It is as if the visual effect itself was not important, which would make no sense at all.

"When I did *She Wore a Yellow Ribbon*, I tried to have the cameras photograph it as Remington would have sketched and painted it. It came out beautifully and was very successful in this respect, I think. When I did *The Searchers*, I used a Charles Russell motif. These were two of our greatest Western artists, of course.

"Is there anything more beautiful than a long shot of a man riding a horse well, or a horse racing free across a plain? Is there anything wrong with people loving such beauty, whether they go to experience it personally, or absorb it through the medium of a movie? Fewer and fewer persons today are exposed to farm, open land, animals, nature. We bring the land to them. They escape to it through us. My favorite location is Monument Valley, which lies where Utah and Arizona merge. It has rivers, mountains, plains, desert, everything the land can offer. I feel at peace there. I have been all over the world, but I consider this the most complete, beautiful and peaceful place on earth. I'm shooting some of *Cheyenne Autumn* there.

"There should never be any shame in liking Westerns," he said. "Westerns are understood and appreciated the world over, as much or more in other countries as here. When I go to Japan, I am more readily recognized and treated more as a celebrity than I am in my own country. When I go to England, I am often paid the respect of being asked to lecture, as I have at Oxford and Cambridge, and am often asked to discuss in particular a film such as *Wagon Master,* which is totally forgotten here. This is all to the good. As a moviemaker, my audience is the world, not just the U.S.

"And if one small segment of the population, the critics, paid and unpaid, professional and amateur, prefer to be snobs and to sneer, I'm certainly not going to worry about it. As long as I can remember these pictures affection- ately and with a little pride, as long as people like them and come to see them, as long as they make money, as long as they are good and honest and attractive and decent films, I'm not going to worry, I'm going to figure they're wrong and we're right."

The Autumn of John Ford

PETER BOGDANOVICH/1964

JOHN FORD WAS BORN Sean Aloysius O'Fearna in Cape Elizabeth, Maine, on the first of February, 1895. His parents had come to America from Galway, Ireland. He directed his first movie in 1917. (It was a two-reeler called *The Tornado,* about a cowboy who rescues the banker's daughter from a gang of outlaws and uses the reward money to bring his Irish mother to the United States. He also played the lead.) The only director to have received six Academy Awards, he is also the only one who has been cited four times by the New York Film Critics. As a Commander in the Navy, he made America's first war documentary, *The Battle of Midway* (1942), as well as *December 7th* (1943), an account of the Pearl Harbor attack and its aftermath; both were awarded Oscars as the best documentaries of their years. Over forty-six years, Ford has made almost a hundred and forty pictures.

One evening he sat up in his bed in Room 19 of Goulding's Lodge. The place was in total disarray. Clothes lay everywhere: on the floor, on tables and chairs, even on the refrigerator. There were also piles of books on every conceivable subject scattered around the room and next to his bed. On it lay a copy of *Gods, Graves, and Scholars.* The little night table was covered with cigars, matches, a watch, pills, glasses, a couple of knives and pencils, loose paper, scripts, and frayed handkerchiefs. Attached to the headboard of the bed was a lamp. The director was discussing movie-making, and you could hear a slight but distinct Maine accent in his speech.

"I love making pictures, but I don't like talking about them," he said,

From *Esquire*, April 1964. 106–7. Reprinted by permission of the author.

cutting a cigar in half with his jackknife. "I mean. Y'know. It's been my whole life. But people ask me which is my favorite—I always say the next one." Raising his arm in the air, he pulled his faded-silk pajama sleeve down. "Y'know. I make a picture and then move on to the next one." He shook his head. "I love Hollywood. I don't mean the higher echelons," he said sarcastically. "I mean the lower echelons, and the grips, the technicians."

After a while, Ford lit a cigar-half and spoke of the difficulty of finding decent stories to do. "My agent," he began, "was at a property conference at one of the studios. And they hold up this book, on the jacket of which was a rather simplified drawing of a nun. He jumped up," Ford said gesturing. " 'My client's a Roman Catholic and that property would interest him very much,' he says." Ford grimaced and chewed on one end of the handkerchief. "I read this thing. It was about a nun who's seduced by a pimp and then falls in love with him. Gets pregnant. She was supposed to run away with him and he told her to meet him at some bridge at one in the morning." He took the handkerchief and held the end a few inches from his mouth. "She went there. Bong! One o'clock. No pimp. You dissolve. Bong, bong. Two o'clock. No pimp. Dissolve again. Three o'clock. So she finally throws herself into the river." The director put the handkerchief back in his mouth. "My agent walked in the door, I threw the book at him," he said, imitating the movement. "I mean Jeez. That's y'know, that's the kinda junk they give you these days." He shook his head.

"Now this thing," he said, nodding at the script of *Cheyenne Autumn* lying on the table, "I've wanted to make this for a long time. Y'know. I've killed more Indians than Custer, Beecher, and Chivington put together." He raised his arm and pulled the sleeve down again. "People in Europe always wanta know about the Indians. They just see them ride by, or they're heavies. I wanted to show what they were like. I like Indians very much," he said warmly. "They're . . . they're a very moral people. They have a literature. Not written. But spoken. They're very kindhearted. They love their children and their animals. And I wanted to show their point of view for a change." Ford pulled down on his cheeks. "S'amazing. . . ." He paused. "It is amazing, working with them, how quickly they catch on despite the language barrier." He rubbed his mouth with the handkerchief.

"But y'know, there's no such thing as a good script. I've never seen one." He paused. "Yes, I have. I've seen *one*. This O'Casey thing I'm gonna do next. Based on his autobiographies. It's the first script I've ever read that I can just go over and shoot." (It was *Young Cassidy*.) He waved his hand in the air. "Well, you know the old thing: one-picture's-worth-a-thousand-words. Scripts are dialogue. I don't like all that *talk*. I try to get things across visually. Y'know, get back to the old thing." He picked up the other half of the cigar and lit it. "I don't like to do books or plays. I prefer to take a short story and expand it rather than take a novel and try to condense." He pulled reflectively on his cheeks. "Producers don't know anything about making pictures," he said earnestly. "And that's why I shoot my films so they can only be cut *one* way." He puffed on his cigar. "They get to the cutting room and they say, 'Well, let's stick a close-up in here.' " Ford paused. "But there isn't one. I didn't shoot it."

The director commented that he'd always wanted to do a stage play. "I like the form," he said and picked up a glass of stale water from the night table. He took a pill from a little box. "B means it's a Bufferin, right?" he said and swallowed the pill. "I once got a letter from the Metropolitan Opera people," he said sardonically. "It was a flowery, purple prose thing. Inviting me to direct *The Girl of the Golden West*. 'Course, they made it very clear I was to have nothing to do with the sets or costumes or the music or. . . ." Ford took the cigar from his mouth, holding his arm up by the elbow. "I wrote back that, first of all, I thought *The Girl of the Golden West* was a *lousy* opera." He paused. "But that I was very interested in directing *La Bohème*." He put the cigar back and puffed on it. "Well, you can imagine, y'know, what they thought of *that!* This dirty old *cow*boy . . . this mangy old . . . wants to do *La Bohème!* Well, I certainly knew more about the Left Bank than the manager of the Metropolitan," he said with a wave of his arm. "They wrote back that they weren't interested in having me do *La Bohème*." He chuckled.

Ford on Ford

GEORGE J. MITCHELL/1964

BECAUSE OF THE IMPORTANCE of John Ford in film history, the recent tribute paid him at the University of California in Los Angeles is worthy of an extended report.

The "tribute" consisted of a panel discussion between Ford, George Sidney, who is president of the Directors' Guild of America, and Hugh Gray, associate professor of theatre arts at UCLA, with Arthur Knight, motion picture curator of the Hollywood Museum, as moderator, and the showing of excerpts from such Ford films as *The Informer, My Darling Clementine* and *The Quiet Man,* and the entire Civil War sequence from *How the West Was Won.*

. . . Ford is a big, shambling man with craggy features and thinning gray hair. He wears heavily framed dark spectacles (a black eye-patch covers the outside of the left lens). He is deaf in his left ear and has a hearing aide in the frame of his spectacles. He appears to have lost a lot of weight and his worn navy-blue jacket hung loosely about his big frame. Underneath he had on a yellow sweater, a soft-collar shirt and a loosely tied dark four-in-hand tie. His well-worn gray flannel trousers were hitched rather high above his waist.

. . . Ford *likes* to tell stories and got rather annoyed—or seemed to—when Moderator Knight interrupted him once or twice in the middle of a good yarn. His stories revealed more about him than his answers to the sometimes pointless questions.

From *Films in Review,* vol. XV, no. 6. June/July 1964. 321–32. © 1964 by *Films in Review.* Reprinted by permission.

Ford had the audience on his side all the way and there was whole-hearted laughter at some of his stories, or, I should say, at the way Ford told them. Occasionally he had the air of a mischievous small boy, as when he would throw a questioner off balance by coming back fast with an unexpected answer. Example: "Mr. Ford, what do you think of Bergman?" Ford, with a wicked smile: "Ingrid? Well, now—oh! You mean *the director* Bergman." He knew all the time the question concerned Ingmar.

Ford was sitting in the front row when Moderator Knight made his introductory speech, in the course of which he mentioned that Ford "had been an actor".

"I deny it," Ford exclaimed. "I just doubled for my brother."

At the conclusion of Knight's remarks, Ford walked slowly and carefully to a chair facing the audience. He removed his glasses and quickly covered his bad eye with the handkerchief that had been hanging untidily out of his breast pocket.

"I woke up today," he explained, "with this damned eye feeling like a bucketful of stilettoes. Maybe, if I'm a good boy, I'll get my glass of medicine when this meeting is over. Can I go home and get it now?"

He lives near the UCLA campus and said gently: "I've been looking at it every day for many years. It has none of the phony Georgian or Renaissance architecture. It's simple—beautiful."

Asked how early in his career he was able to choose the stories he would direct, he said it had been about when he was twenty-six, and that his "first really good story" was *Four Sons* ('28), which was taken from a little story called "Grandma Bernle Learns Her Letters." He added: "Nowadays the son would have to be in love with the mother, or is it his sister?"

When asked about Westerns he replied: "You can't knock a Western. They have kept the industry going. And you can't parody or satirize a Western. I've seen people try—and fail."

Professor Gray asked Ford what sort of stories he like best. "Any good story with a colorful locale that's about human beings," Ford replied. "Anything with interesting characters—and some humor."

Ford does not like "message pictures" and he resisted Knight's attempt to have him say he intended a message of social significance in *The Grapes of Wrath*. When Knight persisted, Ford became impatient.

"I am of the proletariat," he said with some fervor. "My people were peasants. They came here, were educated. They served this country well. I love America. I am a-political."

And that led him to talk about *Cheyenne Autumn,* which he had finished editing a few days before.

"I don't want to sound like I'm plugging it but I *think* it's pretty good," he said. "It's a true story about the Cheyennes and how they outwitted the whole U.S. Army in their retreat across the middle part of this country."

Why had he done this picture?

"I liked the story and caught Jack Warner in a weak moment. He agreed to let me do it. People in Europe and other parts of the world always ask me about the Indians—what they were really like, their culture, their history. I've long wanted to do a story that tells the truth about them and not just a picture in which they're chased by the cavalry. I think we did that in this new picture. I hope we did."

He said he particularly likes *Sergeant Rutledge.* "The colored soldier played a great role in our history," he said, "and I wanted to tell that story. Woody Strode, who went to UCLA here, gave a great performance. But the picture was not successful, because, I've heard, Warners sent a couple of boys on bicycles out to sell it."

Ford was asked about *The Informer* and confirmed the statement attributed to him that it is not one of his favorites.

"I'll tell you about *The Informer.*

"When an old friend named Joe Kennedy, father of the late lamented President, was in control of RKO, he wanted me to work there and he told four or five of RKO's big producers—I know they were big producers because they wore big-check sports coats and smoked big cigars—he wanted them to get me to direct a picture. They informed Joe I didn't want to do a Western but a picture about 'a rebellion in Ireland.' Joe asked how much it would cost. When one of the producers said around $200,000, Joe said: 'Let him make it. It won't lose any more than some of those you've made.' "

When Ford was half way through on *The Informer,* Kennedy disposed of his interest in RKO. "They shut me down for one day and told me they'd have to have the stage I was working on and moved me across Melrose Avenue to the California Studio [now Producers Studio]. Which was good, because they no longer came in each day to tell me how depressing the story was and what a failure the picture was going to be.

"*The Informer* was made in eighteen days and after it was finished they shipped the print to New York and sat on it for about five months. When it was previewed in Hollywood, there were a number of walk-outs. In the lobby of the theatre nobody spoke to me—I was treated like a leper. But when the critics saw it and gave us favorable reviews, things changed. The night the Academy gave it some four Awards, the producer who had opposed it accepted one of them for the studio and made a fifteen-minute speech. He then accepted my Award for Best Direction—and made another fifteen-minute boring speech. He also tried to have his name put on the prints and the advertising, but it was too late for that."

An exerpt from *The Informer* was then shown. It consisted of the last few hundred feet and started with the scene of Gypo being shot down and his death in the church before the mother of the man he had betrayed. Projection was so badly out of focus that Ford exclaimed: "Is this my print?" Assured that it was, he said: "It was a good print the last time I saw it and it was in correct focus."

Professor Gray then asked Ford about Dudley Nichols, who, Gray said, "was deeply loved here at UCLA." Ford replied with feeling: "We were very close. He loved motion pictures. He never used purple prose. He wrote like people speak, and with a minimum of dialogue. He was a wonderful man. I miss him terribly."

He added that no other writer had collaborated as closely with him as Nichols had.

"I like to have the writer with me on the set," Ford continued. "If a scene won't play, the writer can look at it and maybe discover that if he eliminates or adds a word here, or a line of dialogue there, the thing we're striving for can be gotten."

Moderator Knight asked Ford's opinion of those who like only silent pictures and decry their passing. "I am with them," Ford said with some vigor. "I too am a silent picture man. Pictures, not words, should tell the story." Which reminded him of his new picture, and he said *Cheyenne Autumn* "is really a silent picture. It's a true story and I'm rather pleased with it."

The discussion then turned to *The Iron Horse,* a picture Ford obviously wanted to talk about. "I had an Uncle Mike who was in the Civil War," he said proudly. "In fact I had four uncles in the war. I'm a Civil War buff—are there any here in the house? I used to ask my Uncle Mike to tell me about the battle of Gettysburg. All Uncle Mike would say was: 'It was horrible. I went six whole days without a drink.' Uncle Mike was a laborer on the Union

Pacific Railroad when it was built. He told me stories about it and taught me the songs they had sung. I was always interested in the railroad and wanted to make a picture about it."

Fox finally gave him the opportunity, but stipulated a four-week schedule. Ford made a little joke about producers he had worked for who pronounced the word "shed-yool."

"We went up to Wadsworth, Nevada, on the Southern Pacific line where the studio had built sets of a railroad construction crew shanty town. When we got off the train at Wadsworth, it was 20 below zero. I can see those boys and girls from Hollywood now. Some of them had on linen knickers. The Southern Pacific helped a lot and brought in several hundred pairs of long woolen underwear for us. We took the uniforms the studio had sent along as costumes for the soldiers and wore them because they were warm. I remember one girl wore a pair of soldier pants so big it came up around her chin. She cut holes in the side for her arms and didn't care how she looked as long as she was warm.

"The next day it was 25 below and there was a blizzard. I said to George Schneiderman, the cameraman: 'What'll we do? We only have four weeks to make it.' George said there must have been snow when they built the railroad so why don't we shoot anyway? Schneiderman was one of the early cameramen and a great one. He could do anything.

"We lived in passenger cars that belonged to the Al G. Barnes Circus, but some of the people took over the shacks that had been built for the sets and lived in them.

"Despite the bad weather and almost constant exposure to it, no one got sick. I suppose it was being out in the open air that kept them all healthy. Eight of the young men with me became directors, and six or seven of the girls later became important actresses.

"I've begun writing a story about the making of *The Iron Horse*," he said, "and have already finished eight chapters. My wife says it's more pornographic than even current literature. There are some good stories I could tell you—but not in mixed company." The audience was naturally disappointed.

"We had a nice girl named Madge Bellamy, an important star in those days, for the leading lady. After the picture was finished, and I was away on a trip, the studio decided they needed some glamorous close-ups of Madge, so they had an assistant director shoot some. He set the camera up in the bright sunlight and had Madge ooh and ah [Ford mimicked]. When I saw this stuff, I was furious, for it didn't even match the scene it was intended for. But there was nothing I could do."

When Knight and Professor Gray told Ford UCLA was showing *The Iron Horse* the following Thursday evening, he said: "I'd like to see it again, but only if they've cut out those horrible close-ups of Madge."

Gray then asked Ford if it was true, when a production manager complained he was behind schedule, he had once torn pages out of a script and said: "Now we're on schedule!"

"It's absolutely true," Ford answered. "There was this obnoxious little character—I think he was the son of some big shot. He said [Ford mimicked]: 'You're way behind schedule.' He'd been pestering me for days so I tore out ten pages of script and said: 'Now we're three days *ahead* of schedule. Are you happy?' "

Ford became very serious when he talked to the students in the audience about their chances for jobs in motion pictures. "There is nothing we directors can do to give you jobs," he said regretfully. "It's not like it was when I started out and you could walk in and get some kind of a job. It's a terrible situation that exists when young people are denied the opportunity. But, I believe talent is somehow always recognized in the end." And he added with irony: "Of course, if you marry the daughter of some executive producer you'll get to the top fast."

Although fewer pictures were now being made in Hollywood than at any time in the past, Ford said, employment was up because actors and technicians were working on television films and "it was very hard to get a good cameraman now because so many sign up for thirty-nine-week tv shows. It's also hard to get a good gaffer [electrician] and a good grip [stagehand-carpenter-handyman]. Television latches onto all of the good ones. You have to have people who know how to pick it up and put it down where you want it. These gaffers and grips are good—they have to be. I've been very lucky in getting a good crew and a good cameraman."

A student asked if Ford would care to comment on the beautiful photography his pictures always seem to have. "Well," he replied, "I think first as a cameraman, I consider myself a cameraman rather than a director."

George Sidney, who had already described himself as a John Ford fan, remarked that "Mr. Ford never puts in these striking pictorial scenes just for effect. Everything is done to enhance the scene, to tell the story."

Ford rejoined: "It's still a silent medium."

Someone asked if Ford would like to comment on a remark some director had made that "actors are cattle" and if he felt that way. "I can't imagine anyone saying that because the actors I've worked with were real professionals," Ford replied. "They worked hard. I never ran into temperament—not in Americans, anyway."

He parried a question about Ingmar Bergman in the way already described and added: "My eyes are pretty bad and it's difficult for me to look at pictures so I haven't seen any of his, but I understand they're good. I've corresponded with him, and I intend to meet him very shortly on my trip abroad. Perhaps I'll see something he has done then."

Asked what he thought of Akira Kurosawa and whether Kurosawa's Samurai films bore any similarity to Ford's Westerns, he said: "I know him. We consumed a lot of saki together when I was in Japan. He showed me a reel of cut film of his. He has a genuine feeling and works fast. He is a fine director, but I don't think his films are at all like mine."

A student asked if it is true Ford shoots his films so they must be cut his way. Ford smiled and replied: "Yes. Now don't you think that's rather clever?"

Professor Gray asked Ford if he would comment on Ince and his contributions to motion pictures. Ford answered: "He was not really a director, but a producer. My brother [Francis] worked for him but I did not know him. Ince had a great influence on films, for he tried to make the best. But I don't think he was a better film editor than others I've known."

A student asked why Ford did not do more comedies like *When Willie Comes Marching Home* and Ford replied: "I feel I'm essentially a comedy director, but they won't give me a comedy to do. When I direct a scene I always want to make the leading lady fall down on her derriere." He added that though he has more freedom making pictures his way now that he heads his own company, "you still have to deal with bankers and people in New York even if you are your own boss." Knight asked if the company he referred to was Argosy Pictures, a company Ford had formed with Merian C. Cooper, "No," Ford replied wryly, "we dissolved that one *with a capital loss.*"

Knight then alluded to a film called *Sex Hygiene* which Ford directed for the Signal Corps and which all U.S. soldiers of World War II were shown. "I threw up when I saw it," said Ford. Knight described *his* reactions when he saw this film as a soldier. "Did it help you?" Ford airily asked. "Yes," replied Knight.

After an excerpt from *They Were Expendable* was screened, Ford reiterated that he did not like it. He said the Navy had ordered him to leave his outfit overseas to make it, which he did not like. "I knew Johnny Bulkeley [the real life character the story is based on] well. He was a much decorated man, and a brave one. He dropped me on the coast of France several times during the war when I was working with the French underground. I guess it's all right for me to say this, now."

That is the first time, to my knowledge, that Ford has mentioned his work with the OSS during WW II. Ford also remarked in another context: "The Italian Government gave me a medal for blowing up a wrong tunnel."

Asked to comment on the so-called "John Ford stock company" he said: "It's a legend. It's true I've used 'Duke' Wayne, and Ward Bond, God rest his soul, and others, in many pictures, but I don't think of them as a stock company."

"What about Maureen O'Hara?" Knight asked. "Forgive me for that," said Ford, and added: "This is boring." But then added: "I guess I do have a stock company, but it is the many extra and bit players who have worked with me for years. I spend a lot of time with them, more than I do with the main actors."

Before an excerpt from *My Darling Clementine* was screened, Ford declared: "I knew Bill Cody, Pardner Jones, Al Jennings and Wyatt Earp. They used to visit my sets, and were interested in our pictures. I made Henry Fonda play Earp just as he was. Earp was not particularly good with a gun. You really can't shoot a six-gun accurately, you know. Earp was a solemn man and backed them down with his presence. I knew him rather well.

"This is a strange thing to say, but I've never seen *My Darling Clementine*. I hope you are going to show the scene where they dedicate the church. I think that's good."

That sequence was shown, as was the barber shop one in which Fonda gets a haircut and a liberal appliance of hair tonic. When the lights went up and the applause was heavy, Ford said with sincerity: "I enjoyed it."

Before *The Quiet Man* excerpt was shown, Ford had a few things to say about it, and it was evident he likes this picture a great deal.

"This is a very sexy story, you know," he said. "I like good lusty sex but I object to dirty innuendoes. The customs shown in *The Quiet Man* are true and prevail in Connemora, which is the poorest country in Ireland and the only one Cromwell never conquered. I was born in Cape Elizabeth, Maine, but I went to school in Ireland for a while and was brought up to speak both English and Gaelic. Every Irishman is an actor. The Irish and the colored people are the most natural actors in the world.

"*The Quiet Man* was photographed in the rain—or Irish mist, as they call it in Ireland. That helped the picture a lot."

When the questions began to lag Ford, obviously tired, murmured, "You're running out of material" and sat down.

The audience, applauding, rose in his honor. He got up, bowed, resumed his seat, removed his spectacles, and wiped his eye, which several times during the course of the evening had given him pain.

He seemed genuinely moved by the sincerity of the ovation.

John Ford

ERIC LEGUÈBE / 1965

Q : *John Ford, how did you become a director for the cinema?*
FORD : Because I was lucky enough to have a brother who was interested in directing before I was and who introduced me.

Q : *Can you explain?*
FORD : At thirteen years old, I was a delivery boy for a shoe manufacturer. Three years later, my brother Francis had made himself a place in Hollywood, and called me there. I stole the only pair of boots which were a size seven from the shoe manufacturer, and I crossed America to join him. Francis had become a director. The family spirit being one of the attributes of the Irish race, he hired me as an assistant Although he had been born O'Feeney, he had taken the pseudonym Ford. I followed in his footsteps and, for ten years, I was Jack Ford. How much fun we had, Francis and I, actors in the same films, in charge of the same projects!

Q : *John Ford was to take the place of Jack Ford . . .*
FORD : That happened in 1923. From that moment, I bypassed my brother. He was sick with an incurable illness. But I always included him in my projects. He stayed by my side until his death in 1953. Thirty-three years of fraternal love!

From *Confessions 2: A Century of American Cinema.* 37–41. paris IFRANE, 1995. Translated from French by Jenny Lefcourt.

Q : *Do you have a method for directing actors?*
F O R D :   I never had actors to direct, but friends. How could I speak otherwise than in terms of friendship, of fraternity, of people like John Wayne, Victor McLaglen, Henry Fonda? All those who have worked with me have in their memory the phrase which I always repeat during the shooting, during editing: "It's O.K., but it has to be better."

Q : *What are the criteria by which you chose the subjects which you have decided to film?*
F O R D :   I like, as a director and as a spectator, simple, direct, frank films. Nothing disgusts me more than snobbism, mannerism, technical gratuity (that the spectators pay for) and, most of all, intellectualism.

Q : *What place do you give to technique?*
F O R D :   The technique is what you don't see on the screen and which is there to benefit that which the spectators see: the action, the heroes, the characters, the landscape. For me, a film is a success if the spectators leave the theater satisfied, if they identify with the characters, if they get joy or energy.

Q : *You have been given four Oscars in Hollywood, all the festivals in Cannes, Venice . . . tried to jump on the bandwagon that you have led since 1924, with* The Iron Horse. *Of all the awards you have been granted, is there one that you prefer?*
F O R D :   None of that kind. I like the job that I do, I hate the analysis, the evaluation that others permit themselves to have. I am a peasant, and my pride is to remain one.

Q : *What is your fondest memory of the cinema?*
F O R D :   Having been named honorary Sachem by the Navajos, with the name "Great Soldier." People have said that on the screen I like having Redskins killed. But today other people in the cinema feel sorry for them, make humanist pamphlets, declarations of their intentions, without ever, ever putting a hand in a wallet. Myself, more humbly, I gave them work. That is perhaps the reason why, during the shooting of *The Iron Horse,* the chief "Iron Eyes" Cody became my friend. More than having received the Oscars, what counts for me is having been made a blood brother of different Redskin nations. Maybe that is my Irishness, my respect for beauty, clans, in the face of

the modern world, masses, collective irresponsibility. Who, better than an
Irish man, could understand the Indians while remaining enthusiastic about
the fable of the U.S. Cavalry? We are on both sides of the epic. That is what
America was.

Q :   *How would you define yourself?*
FORD :   John Ford, author of westerns, war stories where men count more
than events, and comedies where the strength of feelings counts. Heroism,
laughter, emotion: the rest is just the rest.

Q :   *You aren't only the filmmaker who says "action" for the camera, but you are
also the man of action, the soldier of the Second World War, the marine who participated in the battle of the Pacific and Normandy.*
FORD :   That's why I like Paris so much. One of my greatest memories is to
have beaten a section of the S.S. with my men during a confrontation around
the Caré de la Paix. It wasn't about hate between us, but a fight for different
causes. Similarly, in 1944, I participated in the great events on the parvis of
Notre-Dame. Every time I come to France, I go to pay my respects at Bayeux
on the tombs of French Resistants with whom I was in contact, and at the
cemetery where some of my men were buried.

Q :   *How do you see the evolution of American cinema?*
FORD :   Hollywood, it's over. The new world capitals of cinema from now
on are Paris, London and maybe Rome. In the United States they only have
eyes for television. That is why I am unemployed, or let's say semi-unem-
ployed!

Q :   *But you still have lots of projects?*
FORD :   First of all, I would have liked to devote a film to the great French
aviator, Guynemer. The project is evaporating, without me really renounc-
ing it. But you see, this book, it doesn't leave me. It is the story of the battle
of Lexington. I am working on adapting it, transforming it into a scenario.
     If I do this film, that I see already, I would dedicate most of my work to
the description of the everyday life of those who have today become Americans; to those farmers who began to become attached to this new land, who
then began to revolt against the English soldiers. This aspect of the birth of
the United States, rustic, rough, interests me a lot more than the battle,

John Wayne

Katharine Hepburn and John Carradine, *Mary of Scotland*, 1936

George Bancroft, John Wayne, and Louise Platt, *Stagecoach*, 1939

Henry Fonda and Jane Darwell, *The Grapes of Wrath*, 1940

John Wayne, John Qualen, and Thomas Mitchell, *The Long Voyage Home*, 1940

Charley Grapewin, William Tracy, Elizabeth Patterson, and Gene Tierney, *Tobacco Road*, 1941

Grant Withers, Victor McLaglen, John Wayne, Henry Fonda, George O'Brien, Miguel Inclan, and Dick Foran, *Fort Apache*, 1948

John Wayne and Maureen O'Hara, *Rio Grande*, 1950

John Wayne and Jeffrey Hunter, *The Searchers*, 1956

which is simply the crystallization. I am passionate about this approach to
history. I like to dedicate my films to the little people who suddenly became
conscious that they belonged to a human group, a community. France participated in our War of Independence. Just as it had supported, under Napoleon's directory, the independence of Ireland. That is why I am proud to have
contributed to its Liberation. But I also have a hope that the French will be
interested in my project for a film on the battle of Lexington, which was our
taking of the Bastille.

Q :   *What advice do you have for a beginning filmmaker?*
FORD :   Ask Robert Parrish. He would tell you. After having been my assistant, he took the opportunity to stand on his own feet, (and direct), so he
came and asked my advice. I answered: "Aim between the eyes, like that. . . ."
And I punched him in the nose. Since then, I have seen some of his productions and I saw that he had understood the lesson, his images gave *me* a
punch.

   I am a pioneer, proud to be one. I warn you, despite the love I have for
my profession, I hate to analyze it. To talk about it would give me the impres-
sion never to have done anything.

Q :   *Are there certain of your films which you prefer?*
FORD :   Of course. All of the films in which my friend John Wayne played
the main character. That way I had a nice safety margin! And, *Fort Apache,*
where there is action and humor and where, for the first time, my brothers
of the Indian race are heroes presented in a positive light. And finally, the
last of my feature length films for the moment, *7 Women,* a western that
takes place in China, and in which all the cowboys are women!

Q :   *Do you think the cinema has the right to call itself the Seventh Art?*
FORD :   I hate the cinema. But I like making westerns. What I like in filming
is the active life, the excitement of the humming of the cameras, and the
passion of the actors in front of them, the landscapes on top of that, the
work, work, work. . . . It takes a huge physical effort to remain lucid and not
to fall in the traps of aestheticism and, above all, intellectualism. What
counts is what one does and not what one says. When I make a western, all
I have to do is to film a documentary on the West, just as it was: epic. And
from the moment that one is epic, one can't go wrong. It's the reality, outside

time, that one records on the negative. My biggest pride is not having signed so many films, but having been a cowboy at fourteen. The thirteen dollars that I made represented a bigger fortune than anything I have earned in thousands of dollars from my films. That was when I was rich.

Q: *What do you think of cinema today?*
FORD: I don't go anymore. I don't see why humanity likes that which stresses stupidity and lowliness. Sex, obscenity, violence, ugliness, decadence, degeneration don't interest me. Excesses disgust me. What I like is effort, the will to go beyond oneself. For me, life is to be oneself in the face of friends who you punch in the nose, and then you drink and sing together. It is the attraction to real women, and not the Miss Bovarys. It's the fresh air, the great outdoors, the great hopes.

Filmmakers of Our Time: The Twilight of John Ford

JEAN NARBONI AND ANDRÉ S. LABARTHE/1965

''FORD, FIRST TAKE!''

Freeze frame: Ford in his bed, with a cross on the wall and photographs in frames. Ford, with his famous eye patch, is sitting cross-legged in his pajamas with one hand on his hip, and the other hand holding a cigar which he smokes throughout the interview.

Q: *Monsieur Ford, where do you come from? (kneeling near the bed)*
FORD: (leaning towards the journalist) Portland, Maine.

Q: *Portland, Maine?*
FORD: Well, Peak's Island, Maine. P-E-A-K-S.

Q: *I'm going to ask you a very indiscreet question, when were you born?*
FORD: What is the indiscreet question? Go ahead, ask it first.

Q: *When were you born?*
FORD: Is that indiscreet? I was born in '95. I'm seventy years old. (A woman's voice off camera interrupts: "You are not. You're sixty-eight.")
FORD: Huh? What?

Q: *Sixty-eight?*
FORD: Well, I feel like ninety.

From "Cineastes de notre temps," produced by Hubert Knapp. Printed by permission of Institut National de L'Audiovisuel. Translated from French by Jenny Lefcourt.

Q : *How did you come to the movie pictures? If I may say so . . .*
FORD :   By train. Chemin de fer. (smiles)

Q : *What have you done before making movie pictures?*
FORD :   I am trying to think. I was a cowboy.

Q : *When and where?*
FORD :   Arizona. Before that, I went to school. I got out of school and went West. Finally drifted to Hollywood, got into the . . . I've stayed ever since. 1916.

Q : *But being born in Maine, normally you shouldn't have been a cowboy.*
FORD :   (in French) Why not?

Q : *Because cowboys are people who were . . .*
FORD :   (in French) Sailor, I was a sailor, too.

Q : *(in French) When were you a sailor? At what time?*
FORD :   (in French) During vacation. You know . . . I went to sea. I was a sailor. And I went West to become a cowboy. I washed dishes.

Q : *You what? You washed dishes? In the West?*
FORD :   In restaurants. All the way West.

Q : *How long were you a cowboy?*
FORD :   Oh, about eight months.

Q : *Eight months. How did you like it?*
FORD :   I liked it very much. The pay was poor.

Q : *So you had to quit. No money.*
FORD :   No, no. I just wanted to move on, I was restless and moved on.

Q : *And after that?*
FORD :   I went to Hollywood.

Q : *Being what first?*
FORD :   A laborer, with a pick and shovel. Then I became a propman, assistant director, and eventually a director. I started directing when I was nineteen.

Q : *When you were nineteen! Which year was it? Oh yes, it was in . . .*
F O R D :   That later part of '16. Then the war came along, of course. And afterwards I came back and I continued directing.

Q : *What was the first picture you directed when you were nineteen?*
F O R D :   (in French) I don't know.

Q : *The first picture you made after the war, what was it?*
F O R D :   I don't know!

Q : *I meant after the war!*
F O R D :   (in French) I don't know, old man! (in English) I don't know!

Q : *And what is the first picture you remember?*
F O R D :   (smile crosses his face) I don't remember. *The Iron Horse.*

Q : *It was about the construction of the train?*
F O R D :   (indicates his glass, in French) Spanish wine tastes good, doesn't it? It's very good.

Q : *Yes, very good.*
F O R D :   (in French) It's better than what they make today. Ginger ale. (laughs) Go ahead. Continuez, continuez. Continuez en anglais. Si'l vous plaît.

Q : *I'll try. I'll try my best.*
F O R D :   (in French) I have forgotten everything. I am very, very deaf.

Q : *(in French) In French you are a little deaf.*
F O R D :   Yeah, fighting for France. (smiles)

Q : *In English you are not.*
F O R D :   (in French) A wound in France.

Q : *Monsieur Ford, you have lived almost the whole of the American history of the movie picture.*
F O R D :   True.

Q : *When you look back, how do you feel about it? What do you feel about the way it was done?*

FORD: Well, if I wanted to live my life over again, I would still do the same thing. Hollywood, I mean, has a bad press. They're wonderful people, the most noble, a lot of people, the most charitable. They have the best record, for example the best military record, of any industry in the country. The best civil record and the best charitable record. Of course, some star, or somebody who pretends to be a star, gets in trouble, you have headlines in *Le soir* (draws a headline in the air) . . . not *Le soir,* what's the other? No, but . . . we have a bad press, but they are magnificent people. Charitable, kind, nice, very nice. It's the people that you get the scandal from, some of them are not even in the business.

Q: *And when you think of the first pictures you made here . . . what did you think you would achieve when you made your first pictures?*
FORD: I thought I would achieve a check. For money. That's all I thought about.

Q: *And when did you start thinking that there was something more than checks behind it?*
FORD: This is my business, my profession, it's the way that I support my family. I love the business; I like the people; I am not what is called a "career director."

Q: *What do you mean by that?*
FORD: Some men will make a good picture then they keep on trying. They won't work for a year and a half; they're trying to beat the last one. I just keep on going making pictures, good, bad, indifferent. I just like to be around the studios. I like the people I work with. I'm absolutely without ambition. I have no ambition. I like pictures. I like to make pictures.

Q: *Mr. Ford, you pretended not to be interested after you have made a film, a picture, by this picture. Is that right?*
FORD: "Pretend" is very rude.

Q: *I'm sorry.*
FORD: I think of the next picture.

Q: *You think of the next picture. But does it happen that among the tens—can you say "tens?"—of pictures you made, does it happen that there is one, or two, or several, which you particularly like?*
FORD: (silence) Yes, but you've never heard of them.

Q : *Yes, why?*

FORD : They were little pictures. They didn't make any money, but lost money, no stars, but they came out perfectly for me. None of the big pictures . . . you know . . .

Q : *Can you name one?*

FORD : *Young Mr. Lincoln, The Sun Shines Bright.*

Q : *He knows them (gestures to other journalist).*

FORD : I like them.

OTHER JOURNALIST : *Yes, I like too.*

FORD : Let's shake hands. (In French) You are very nice.

OTHER JOURNALIST : *What about* The Searchers?

FORD : Just a Western.

OTHER JOURNALIST : *A good Western!*

FORD : No, just a Western.

Q : *You know, we have lots of people in France interested by the movies, who think that the Western is a very important part of the moving pictures. Many intellectuals think it's the expression of the American soul.*

FORD : Well, the Western is the best type of picture that's action, mostly true, all this has happened. But you have horses, you have movement, you have background, scenery, color. And that's why they're interesting. I think most of our best pictures are Westerns. I can imagine the French intellectuals liking them. I like them!

Q : *It's often been said that you have sort of your own stock company of actors, is that true?*

FORD : No, that isn't true. No, that's just a legend. I use anybody. But for extras I try to use the same people. They know exactly what I want, they do as I tell them, and they're very grateful.

Q : *Monsieur Ford, is there a particular way of directing your actors when you make a Western?*

FORD: Um, um. (Leans back on his bed with one leg up.) It's the same. You find that every cowboy's a good actor. You pick 'em out, they can speak the line just as well as any other actor. They're all trained. And they're not afraid. They just get up and speak their minds and they're good.

Q: *So why use professional actors?*
FORD: Well, they are professional actors.

Q: *Oh. Why very often in your pictures do the women . . . they are so often getting a little . . . over the behinds.*
FORD: I don't understand. Behind. You mean la derrière?

Q: *Why are they beaten by men? Why are they being punished?*
FORD: Who?

Q: *Women.*
FORD: Where?

Q: *In your pictures.*
FORD: What picture?

Q: Donovan's Reef, *for example.*
FORD: Oh, the audiences like it. I've only done it twice. I adapt that from the French, from the "Apache," they're always beating their women, see? That's an influence I get from the French. They are always scouring their women with knives.

Q: *And* The Quiet Man.
FORD: Well, that was funny. You don't think that was amusing?

Q: *Oui, very funny.*
FORD: (claps hands) Au revoir, mes amis. I've got to have dinner! I eat, you know. I've been working all day.

Ford on Ford 1

AXEL MADSEN/1966

OUR MEETING WITH JOHN Ford took place in a big colonial-style house, where he lives with his wife, his grandson, and a Finnish couple who are the domestics. He was flat out with a flu, which already had knocked out the rest of his family. In sky-blue pajamas and a Scottish scarf, he was sitting rather than lying on his bed, smoking endless cigars (which he lit with enormous kitchen matches). He was tired but sharp-spirited, moving, ironic.

AXEL MADSEN: *Are you planning any movies?*
JOHN FORD: I'm reading a lot of stories. I was out there in Honolulu reading a pack of scripts about six foot high, and they were all filth, dirty. And I don't know . . . it's against my conscience and my religion. I'm not constituted to make that kind of picture, really stupid. They say that's what the audience wants, sex and violence. I don't agree.

M: *What do you look for in a script?*
F: Oh, I like a simple story, but two stories I'm working on are not simple. One is a present-day Navy story, and the other is set in Pakistan between World War I and World War II. If I do the Navy story, I'll have to go up to Alaska and do it. For the other, I'd have to go to Pakistan, and I've traveled enough.

Interviewed March 14, 1966. © 1966 Axel Madsen. Ford's original English has been retained. Reprinted by permission of the author. Translated from Danish by Jan Lumholdt.

M :   *When you first came to LA, your brother, Francis, was already here as a direc-*
tor and actor.
F :   *Lucie Love* was a serial my brother was doing, and I was an assistant prop
man, and I doubled for him. I drove off bridges, jumped the horses off cliffs.
I was right out of starting college and I was fairly athletic.

M :   *What was the prerequisite to becoming a director in those days?*
F :   When I first came out here, the directors were a closely knit club, very,
very, tight, and it was hard to break in. Not any more! They hire them off
the street in New York and send them here. Some guy comes in from Czecho-
slovakia and they give him an office. Oh, it's very easy to become a director
now, as long as you're not American or as long as you don't belong out here.
But in those days, directors were great men. They wouldn't speak to anybody,
very pompous. They had to get their money in cash. No checks.

M :   *Did you know Cecil B. De Mille?*
F :   He was a very strange character, a very charming man, very nice, and a
great, great showman. He's probably our greatest showman.

M :   *If it was so hard to become a director, how did you manage?*
F :   An assistant director quit and I stepped up. That's when they first opened
Universal City. Mr. (Carl) Laemmle came out (from New York) through the
Panama Canal and the place was crowded and they put on great shows. And
they had a grand ball on the one permanent stage with a roof on it, and we
the assistants had to act as bartenders. This party went on and on and finally
about six in the morning I got tired and I dug under the bar and went to
sleep. I woke up about eight and I knew we'd have to shoot that day. We had
a crowd, cowboys, a village, and a back street. But none of the directors (including Francis) showed up. They were suffering, you know, . . . what is the
French for "hangover"?
      But anyway, I was waiting there with the cowboys and the manager rides
up and says, "Mr. Laemmle is coming with a couple of hundred people. For
heaven's sake! Pretend you're Francis and start to do something." Well, I
didn't look enough like Francis to do something, but I had a cowboy ride
through the streets shooting. So the manager says, "Do something else." So
I pointed to three boys and said, "As you come through the street, you fall
there, you fall there, and you fall there." And they rode through the streets

and "BOOM," fell, because there were a lot of pretty girls in the crowd. Now, a horse fall is $250. Then you were paid an extra dollar.

Bernie, Mr. Bernstein, who was the manager, said, "Keep on going." So I said (to the cowboys), "As you ride through this town, I'm going to fire a shot—there's a big crowd of Indians out there shooting at you—and more of you people fall." I was shouting through a megaphone. I fired a shot and every cowboy, I think there were about fifty of them, fell off horses. Well, they (watching) all thought that was great. I said, "Holy Moses." Bernie said, "What can you do now?"

I said, "How much does this village cost us?" "Just wood," he said. So what I did was got hold of some kerosene and poured it over the village, set the village on fire, and had the cowboys ride back and forth through it shooting. Finally, there was no more village and everybody had to leave. And so a month later, they needed a director to direct Harry Carey. Mr. Laemmle said, "What's the matter with Jack Ford? He's a good director. He yells real loud." They said, "He's an assistant." He said, "He's good. Give him a chance." I was getting $50 a week as an assistant. They cut me to $35 a week and I became a director. That's how it all started."

M :   *And that was, I believe,* Cactus, My Pal?
F :   The first picture I did was called *Sky Pilot. Cactus, My Pal?* I've never heard of that.

M :   *Do you remember* The Scrapper? The Soul Herder? Straight Shooting?
F :   *The Soul Herder! That* was the first picture I made! With Harry Carey.

M :   *And that's where you got $35 a week.*
F :   And Harry Carey was getting $75. His contract was running out and that's why they put me to direct him. They didn't care, you know? We made one picture a week, and Carey and his wife went back East and met a friend there in the accounting department of Universal. And suddenly he found out that he was their biggest seller, the biggest moneymaker on the lot. So he went from $75 to $1500 a week, and I went to $75.

M :   *Describe those Harry Carey movies.*
F :   Instead of doing ordinary Westerns, we did them a little differently. Carey didn't have chaps. He'd dress like a real cowboy. We'd write the stories

ourselves and we had a lot of humor in them, we had fun with them. The stories were not the kind you see on television. The characters were real characters, and we had a good bunch of cowboys with us.

M : *What's the silent picture of yours you like best?*
F : Oh, I wouldn't remember. I think *Four Sons,* probably.

M : *And what happened when sound came in?*
F : Nothing. We just made them with sound.

M : *But there must have been a big transition.*
F : Yes, I guess there was quite a transition. We silent directors, we all got our notices or they tried to buy out our contracts at about one tenth of what they were worth. So we all struck and said, "We'll report every week, see? Draw our salaries." They imported a lot of New York stage directors and those pictures were awful, and halfway through they started calling us, "Would you finish this up?" They'd say, "None of the oldtimer (actors) can talk." God, anybody can talk! So they got rid of the New York directors and we just went on making pictures.

My first sound picture was called *Napoleon's Barber.* I was showing Josephine on her way to Waterloo and her coach had to go over a bridge. The soundman and everybody raised the dickens: "You can't go outside and make sound. You gotta go inside. You can't do this and you can't do that." And I said, "Let's try it." So we went outside and had Napoleon saying, "What is the name of that village near Brussels called something?" And it turned out perfectly, so everybody went outside. It's much easier making pictures with sound. The problem was developing writers who knew dialogue.

M : *Who is the screenwriter you are most fond of?*
F : Dudley Nichols, who passed away.

M : *What was remarkable about him?*
F : I didn't say he was remarkable. He was a good, sound, hardworking, dedicated writer, and if you wanted to help him, he'd accept your help. If you gave him an idea and he didn't like it, he'd say so. But if he liked it, he'd work hard on it, and he had a very good story sense. So we got along all

right. We were very good friends. We used to go fishing together, which is
more important than making pictures.

M :   *When were you first in France?*
F :   Let's forget that.

M :   *In World War I?*
F :   Yeah, but I didn't see a hell of a lot of France. Coming into St. Nazaire,
they wouldn't let you off the boat. The last time wasn't too long ago. I went
over to Bayeux on the coast to put some flowers on the graves of some of the
boys I lost. Pretty city, Bayeux. . . . I don't like Paris, you know. I like Carca-
sonne, Avignon, Fontorelle. I was in Fontorelle when we liberated it with
Patton's army. We were in front of a church, and one of the nuns asked,
"Etes-vous Anglasi?," and I answered, "The hell I am! Je suis Americain." The
abbess asked if I was Catholic. Since I answered affirmatively, I was asked to
light the first candle of the Liberation in the abbey. It was one of the high-
lights my life.

M :   *Of your sound films before* Stagecoach, *which do you remember best?*
F :   *Submarine Patrol.* That was a comedy, that was fun. And *The Plough and
the Stars.* Well, I got mad at that one. I finished it and took my boat and
sailed to Honolulu, and a new boss at the studio had an assistant director
take ten days of retakes on it. Instead of having the two leads married, they
were "sweethearts." They were on the same bed, but sweethearts, you see.
Screwed it all up. But I understand there was a terrific fuss about it from the
Irish—it took place in Dublin—and in Europe, and they put it back the way
I made it.

M :   *Did they often tamper with your pictures?*
F :   Oh yes, Jesus! There's nothing you can do about it. You can raise hell,
you can throw bricks through windows, but it's still in the contract that they
want with them. George Stevens is suing the TV people. Do you know anything about that? I wouldn't look at a picture of mine on TV. Just as you're
moving into something, they cut to a dame in a bathtub, detergents. It's
awful. About twenty years ago, I started to look at *Stagecoach* on TV, but every
time it got interesting they cut to a commercial. . . . I'm an awfully poor

person to interview about pictures. I'm not particularly interested in them. I make them and leave them alone. I walk away from them.

M :   *Why are you so famous then?*
F :   I don't know. Luck. . . . Did they ever do a story about Guynemer, the famous ace in World War I?

M :   *They're doing one in Ireland now,* The Blue Max, *about a World War I German ace.*
F :   And they're doing that in Ireland? A Kraut? That's funny.

M :   *What about the film they finished for you there?* Young Cassidy?
F :   Well, I hardly started when I came down with double pneumonia. I was down to 139 pounds, now I'm up to 188 and I can't get it off. . . . They offered me one of those French flying pictures, but that's something I don't know about. I'm a sailor, not a flier. What I remember about fliers is that they came into Paris and all they were doing was drinking, dames, and parties. Christ, it was a beautiful war! . . . But I want to do something I know. I'm an old submariner. Je suis un vieux matelot. My accent is very Norman. We had a lot of French-Canadians where I grew up and they spoke very pure, old Norman.

M :   *How about Indian languages?*
F :   I picked up a lot of Navajo. My verbs aren't that good, but I can understand a lot of it, and I can direct them. The trouble was that they would never speak to me in English, they'd always speak to me in Navajo. There were interpreters but they weren't very good.

M :   *What did the Indians think of your movies?*
F :   They'd never see movies except when we were down there. We'd bring down a picture they worked on and show it to them in a tent. Oh, they'd sit there and enjoy it very, very much. They were kind of startled at first, but they liked them. Comedy they wouldn't understand, but a western would appeal, something with action.

M :   *It seems that in* Cheyenne Autumn, *you tried to show their side of things.*
F :   I didn't try. I *did.* That's a true story. The American government were the heavies, and it showed exactly how it happened, how everything promised

was broken. . . . I love to shoot down there, on the Navajo reservations, and I'm really the only one they let shoot on their sacred grounds, where the dead are buried, scenes of their heroic battles. I'm actually an adopted chief of the tribe: Natani Nez.

They've never been defeated, you know? The other tribes were afraid of them. They're very quiet peacable people, but in battle they're terrific riders and very brave. In World War II, a lot of Navajos were in the Navy and they'd use them as beach masters. They were the ones who translated from the ship to the beach what to do. The Japanese couldn't break down the Navajo language, so they could speak out in Navajo, "Send the second wave," and so forth. They're great people. I go down there on vacation instead of to Palm Springs or Las Vegas. If I have a few days, I go down to Monument Valley and it's very pleasant, solitude.

M :   *When you shoot a western, how do you decide where to put the camera?*
F :   I say, this is the best shot here, let's put the camera here. You don't do that ahead of time, you do it the day you're shooting.

M :   *But how do you know it's this spot and not that spot?*
F :   I don't know. You do it by instinct. I mean, here's a river and a tree and in the background mountains and over there flats, so you shoot the prettiest. You shoot what would look best on screen. Experience, instinct. That's it.

M :   *And what's the important thing about actors?*
F :   You want someone who fits the character. You like to get a nice person who'd be fun around the set. When I work, I work very hard, but we always have a lot of fun.

M :   *Do you often do many takes?*
F :   No, very few takes. I rehearse in a rehearsing room.

M :   *Just around a table?*
F :   Yes, and we rehearse and rehearse until we get it fine. Meanwhile, they are lighting the set and arranging things and when they're ready we come out. And they run through it once or twice and I usually make it in one, two, three shots. If it runs over three shots, I bring (the actors) back into the re-

hearsal room. The scene isn't going well, what can we do with it? Maybe if you add a line or cut one out there, it helps.

In the old days, you used to go out and make pictures. Now you may pick a story and present it to the head of the studio. He sends it off to New York. They make a synopsis that's read before a board, and it's given to the board members. Now you know the board members aren't going to read it, so they give it to their wives. See? So, Jesus, now it's going from here to there and God knows who reads the story.

I've just had one of the best scripts I've ever had, I worked on it for seven months, and I finally got word back from the office that it was too soft. "Not enough sex and violence." A beautiful story, one I really liked. With comedy, pathos, nice characters. No heavies, no shooting, just very nice. "Too soft." So I got furious and I said, "Take your studio and stick it!" Now you have to wait, and they come to you with these silly goddamned scripts. There's one over here: on the first page, a soldier rapes a twelve-year-old Indian girl, on the second page, the Indians catch him and castrate him. This is great for me, my type of work!

The British are making pretty good pictures nowadays. They do good stories that don't necessarily have sex and violence. They know one thing, how to laugh at themselves.

M : *How about the Italians? They make good movies. Fellini's pictures?*
F :   I've never seen one, but I understand that. We couldn't attempt anything like that here, of course. In Hollywood, there's always the economic question. The oldtime directors try to keep their salaries up and the new boys work for nothing. Now I know at MGM there's a bunch of boys preparing stories. They're not getting paid. If MGM accepts a story, *then* they get paid. But you know, people like Capra, Leo McCarey, they're not going to work for that kind of money. They want us to cut our salaries, we'd rather retire. To hell with them! We've got more money than they have! (Laughter.)

M : *In the old days, there was money in the movie business. I remember reading that Tom Mix got $10,000 a week, and that was before there was income tax.*
F :   That's true. Bill Farnum also got it. And in cash. They wouldn't accept checks. Tom probably didn't know what a check was. They'd have to pay him ten $1,000 bills every week. And he spent it all and he died broke. Mary and I knew him very well. (Calling to his wife) Mary! Did Tom die broke?

MRS. FORD: No, he had $6,000 in his pocket and a 24 carat diamond in his belt buckle, which he always said was his fare home, no matter where he went.

F: But he didn't leave a fortune. Except for what (his wife) Vicky got, of course.

MRS. FORD: She got over a million dollars in jewelry. I remember one day when he gave Vicky $125,000. For her birthday.

F: That's a helluva present.

MRS. FORD: He adored me. There never was a Mother's Day without him sending me a telegram no matter where he was in the world. He said in the telegrams, "The other 364 days of the year belong to the world, but today is yours." He never sent his wife one. She said to him once, "How come you're always sending Mary one, but you never send me one?" And he said, "You're not the type!" (Laughter.)

F: He was a terrific guy, Tom. And he was very easy to work with, as long as he knew what he was doing, his capabilities. He'd get out there and do some stunts, he'd work like hell, then he'd sit back and let his crew take care of everything. He enjoyed making pictures.

M: *And you directed how many of them?*

F: Quite a few. Don't ask me the names.

M: *Did you know Bronco Billy Anderson?*

F: I'm not that old. Jesus Christ, I'm only seventy! That was back in 1908. I was in short pants then.

M: *But you did know D. W. Griffith?*

F: Oh, sure. When he was doing *The Birth of a Nation,* I worked three days as a Klansman. I worked as an extra, that's all. Later I knew him quite well. A very fine gentleman. And he certainly pulled the business on his feet. He died broke, though. We all die broke.

M: *Did you ever cut your pictures yourself?*

F: In the old days, you had to cut your pictures. I mean manually. Now you just supervise. "Put that back in, cut that out." Not that it makes a difference, they change them anyway. . . . How did *The Greatest Story Ever Told* turn out?

M: *It didn't make any money.*

F: Biblical stories . . . I don't know, are pretty dull. They all forget that Christ was a human being. A man. Who was the first American saint? Mother something. They were talking to me about a movie, and I said, "Don't get a Catholic to do it. I'm a practicing Catholic. I would treat it with too much respect." She was a woman, a human being. "Get someone who is an atheist or a Protestant or a Jew to make it."

M: *A picture that's loved very much in France is* The Man Who Shot Liberty Valance, *which was sort of a "Fordian" picture: clean, clear, simple.*

F: Fordian?

M: *Yes.*

F: Oh, Fordesque.

M: *You know the famous film critic, Andre Bazin. Do you know he wrote beautiful things about you? (Quotes from a Bazin article, "A la veille de la guerre.")*

F: That's very nice. (Pause) Did you ever go to Bayeux?

M: *No, but I know they make tapestries.*

F: They don't. They did at the time of William the Conquerer. The Tapestry of Bayeux. I went there right after the War, and everything was locked up. It was all these Resistance fighters, and we just had a big lunch and we were full of wine and food. We knocked at a door, and this guy took us down into his cellar, and there in a safety box he had this tapestry. Then he showed us what he swore was the sword of William the Conqueror. He was making fun of us.

M: *Did you do any shooting during D-Day?*

F: I had to lead them ashore. Yes, I was one of the first men ashore. My luck, my boat was one of the first to land.

M: *On the 6th or 7th of June?*

F: The 6th. At the first hour, I had these boys, got them placed. Told them to keep their heads down behind the dunes and photograph, and we filmed the second wave of ships. Bellevue-sur-Mer, I think that's what the spot was called. We got lucky, and I didn't lose one of my guys, at least not there.

M :   *Did you see* The Longest Day?

F :   No, I wouldn't want to. Because it's not a true story of the invasion. Zanuck made it. That's the way people believe it was, thousands of people coming ashore. It wasn't like that. There were groups of thirty or forty, fighting their way up. First we had to knock out the SS.

M :   *You made films for the Navy during the War.*

F :   Yes, and two, *The Battle of Midway* and *December 7th,* won Academy Awards. *The Battle of Midway* I photographed by myself. I had nobody with me. I happened to be there.

M :   *You know about F-stops and ASA numbers?*

F :   Oh, sure. I'm a helluva cameraman. It was my job to sort of look out when the attack came. All I had was an IMO, a little 16mm camera, and I kept changing and changing the magazines and putting them in my pocket. I got wounded badly.

M :   *But the film was saved.*

F :   Yes, but it jumped at places. It's been done a lot of times since; they fake it, making the camera shake. But it happened naturally (to me) because the explosions were so close.

M :   *Your first film after the War was* They Were Expendable *about the real-life Lt. John Bulkeley.*

F :   There's a picture of him in the den, our most decorated hero. He's the one who got MacArthur out of the Phillipines. He's still a great friend of mine. Each time I had to go to France, he'd come out with a whole flotilla of PT boats and say, "I'll take you in."

M :   *What do you think about color photography?*

F :   I prefer black and white. It's much easier to photograph in color. You have to be a real cameraman to photograph in black and white. But the company says, "It must be in color."

M :   *And what about producers?*

F :   We directors don't know what the producer does. People say, "Who is producing your latest film?", and I say, "I don't know, I've never met him."

(Laughing). We don't pay any attention to him. He's not even an accountant. He sits and looks at the rushes, you know? And tells you how it should
have been done, how he wants it. I say, "Go out and do it," and he says, "I
don't know anything about it."

M : *And music?*
F : I didn't care for the music in *The Fugitive.* It sounded like Cossack music.
I'm fond of music, but when two people meet in pictures the philharmonic
orchestra has to go into it. A few simple phrases, yes, but too much music!
You can't hear the dialogue.

M : *They say you hardly ever use dolly shots.*
F : I do, but very gently and slowly. You don't notice them. I like to keep
the audience's attention on [my people's] eyes.

M : *How about your latest film,* 7 Women?
F : The company didn't like it. No stars. But I thought Maggie, what the hell
is her name? . . . Margaret Leighton. I thought she was great. I think it's one
of my best-directed pictures, but it didn't appeal to the public. That's not
what they wanted.

The Old John Ford Talks about Westerns

MICHELE MOTT/1966

JOHN FORD, DIRECTOR OF the most beautiful westerns in the world, is in Paris. He has come to preside over the re-release of *Fort Apache*. Rediscovering Paris, Notre Dame, and the benefits of leisurely walks, he made the acquisition of a cane ahead of time.

Then he came back to his hotel. That's where I found him. He had taken refuge in his bed, which seemed to occupy entirely his large body, covered in freckles, his yellow hair standing up on his head. He began by telling me that he was a Vice Admiral, an officer of the Legion of Honor, decorated with a "croix de guerre." I told him that in France he incarnated the western above all.

Q: *Mr. Ford, what do you think of the new version that has just been made of* Stagecoach?
A: It's disgusting. Why make a new film when the first is still a huge success in the entire world? With all due modesty, I would say that the film you are talking about isn't any good at all.

Q: *Do you feel the same about the new ensemble of actors?*
A: I, who directed John Wayne, Henry Fonda, James Stewart, Victor McLaglen, the old guard. . . . The old were much better. They knew how to do everything: to play a comedy, to inhabit a character, and at the same time,

From *Paris-Presse l'intransigeant,* July 12, 1966. © 1966 by France-Soir. Reprinted by permission. Translated from French by Jenny Lefcourt.

to ride a horse, to be a good shot, to accomplish a physical performance. It's much harder to work with young people: those who know how to act are rare.

Q :   *Still, you have a good school in the United States. The Actors Studio.*
A :   I don't understand what you are saying.

Q :   *The Actors Studio and Elia Kazan.*
A :   I don't know anything about it. I don't know anything about my friend Kazan's activities. You can't learn how to act. It's innate. It's inside you. Did Sacha Guitry go to school? And Claude Dauphin? And Jean Gabin? By the way, what's become of him? Him, he played with his heart.

Q :   *And according to your heart, could you give a definition of the western?*
A :   It's a film in which you work with nice people and in nature. You eat delicious things, you put up tents in the prairie. You have fun. It's nice.

Q :   *Still, the western is something besides this epicurism. In* Fort Apache, *you take the Indians' side and demystify the American general that Henry Fonda incarnates.*
A :   I am not trying to make a legend live. I simply recall historic facts. Because it is based on American history, on people who existed, the western moves me. Did you know that Fonda went to the location to gather material before playing the role of the mean general?

Q :   *Is the western still the rage in the United States?*
A :   Americas, especially New Yorkers, go to see French films. They come out of the cinema swooning and repeating, "It's marvelous!" They want above all to appear very sophisticated. But children adore westerns. . . . We will continue, we must continue, to make western-style films.

Q :   *In France we like westerns a lot. In Spain and Italy, they actually make them as well.*
A :   Oh really? I didn't know that. But it seems to me that you have to be American in order to express the spirit of the pioneers, to discover the Far West. The western is only for us Americans. Why don't the French do the

story of Guynemer, the best aviator in the world? That would be a project I'd like to do if I were French.

And George Washington? Who cares about George Washington? It can't be left up to the French to make a film about him. It's up to me. (He smiles, and straightens his eye patch.) I should be retired by now. But that bores me, retirement. So, I'll settle for a little film that will make me happy. No, no more big films.

And John Ford, soothed, lies back on his bed, crushing his pillow.

Télérama's Exclusive Interview with John Ford in the Flesh

CLAUDE-JEAN PHILIPPE/1966

WHEN I ARRIVE IN the lobby of the Royal Monceau at five o'clock, Pierre Rissient and Bertrand Tavernier, the press representatives, are pessimistic.

Ford has just politely dismissed a colleague after a few minutes of discussion. He decided to sleep. I will thus wait three hours for him to wake up. That brings us to 8 PM. And we'll still have to see if he's willing to receive me. As a journalist, I don't have a chance. Bertrand Tavernier will introduce me as a personal friend.

At eight o'clock, the old pirate wakes up. Everyone is bustling about his bed, lavishing attention on him. I enter on tiptoe. I am introduced. Hand shake. John Ford in his pajamas, hoary, clean-shaven, blotchy, smoking a cigar while feeling his prominent stomach. He is impassive like a Tibetan bronze sculpture. . . . He smokes cigar after cigar, perfectly relaxed. He asks to shave. He is brought a razor, a mirror, and shaving cream. He shaves in front of us, without modesty, simply. It's as if we were in a Texas fort, in the middle of a scene in the barracks.

He resolutely refuses to talk cinema. As soon as there's talk of one of his films, he scowls and pretends never to have seen it. Everyone is surprised, provokes him, even accuses him of lying. Nothing helps. John Ford hasn't seen John Ford's films. And when, by chance, he sees one on television, the program is so packed full of commercials that he turns off the set.

From *Télérama*, July 31–August 6, 1966. Reprinted by permission of the author. Translated from French by Jenny Lefcourt.

But in a way, without meaning to, he is constantly talking about his films. The themes of his conversation are those of his work, beginning with Ireland, family, travel, intermingled motifs in his life and films.

He dreams out loud: "The sea . . . I was brought up close to the sea. If I hadn't been a director, I would have been a sailor."

John Ford has a yacht which is his second home. So I ask: "Do you like to travel?"

"No," he answers, "I have traveled too much. I have seen every country in the world as far as Tibet. Now I prefer staying home."

"You often evoke the war. Is this because you like it?"

John Ford throws up his arms. Then the answer comes after some time: "So you know another way to leave home for a while?"

His turn to ask us a question: "Does the army in France have a political influence? In the United States, the American Legion, which rallies all the veterans, is very powerful."

"Do you approve of this intervention of the military in political life?"

"No, not at all. It could be very dangerous."

If the accusation of militarism amuses him, that of racism makes him jump.

"I am the first," he says, "to have made a black the main character of a western (*Sergeant Rutledge*). How could I be a racist, me who saw so many black soldiers fall on the beaches of the Normandy landing? I consider the blacks to be full-fledged American citizens."

John Ford is open about his religious sentiments. The journalist who came before me represented *l'Humanité*. When he learned that it was a Communist journalist, Ford asked for his rosary to give to the unbeliever.

"I am Irish," he tells me, "thus, Catholic. This doesn't stop me from being anticlerical. One can be a fervent Catholic and hate sermons. I choose my priests like I distribute my films." Let's note that the next day, Sunday, John Ford will attend the mass at Notre-Dame of Paris.

Four hours have passed, interspersed with laughter and even songs, those Irish ballads which the marvelous old man hums with a hoarse voice. John Ford invites us to have dinner with him. He eats egg casserole accompanied by a Bordeaux. One should see the mischievous patience with which he holds out his glass while he waits for it to be filled to the rim. Like his characters, he drinks bottom-up.

The Fourth Dimension of Old Age

CLAUDINE TAVERNIER/1966

WHEN HE ARRIVED, WE accosted him like one accosts a sage.

We sat around his bed, our chin in the palm of our hand, a hungry stare fixed on him. We were waiting for him to speak. Because in our country, artists are voluble. They explain, they explain a lot of very interesting things, very complicated, very intelligent, we ruin our fingers writing down their words. But this one doesn't speak.

Not bothered by our stares either, he remains there, sitting on his bed calmly smoking his cigar. The ashes fall on the sheets.

FORD: I don't know myself. All these people who come to interview me know a lot more about my films than I know myself. In Hollywood, we don't talk much about cinema. When we shoot, we start very early, because we live very far from the studios and we have a long way to travel. And in the evening, we go home. We all live pretty far from one another. Duke Wayne lives more than fifty kilometers from my house. That is why we don't get together very often. And as soon as we have finished a film, we head far off from Hollywood, some for Honolulu, others for New York. . . . When I am alone, I read a lot. Mostly history books. I love history. I probably know the history of France better than all of you.

Q: *Who are your favorite writers?*
FORD: Liam O'Flaherty, who was my cousin, Edward Morrow when he writes, Frances Parkinson Keyes, Balzac, the Russian novelists, Conan Doyle.

From *Cinéma,* no. 137. June 1969. Reprinted by permission of the author. Translated from French by Jenny Lefcourt.

Once a year I reread *The Three Musketeers*. I hate Hemingway. Faulkner isn't bad.

Q : *Since you say you never heard so much talk about the cinema, what do you talk about with your friends?*

He punctuates his words, always implacably serious.

FORD : We talk about baseball and sex. Mostly about baseball.

We laugh. He doesn't laugh.

Q : *Do you never laugh?*
FORD : Yes, I laugh all the time. But inside.

He likes asking abrupt questions, and suddenly asked Claude-Jean Philippe if his father was a peasant, and to Bertrand Tavernier:

FORD : Are you superstitious?

BERTRAND TAVERNIER : No, and you?

FORD : Yes. I decided to be two years ago.

BERTRAND TAVERNIER : Why?

FORD : It adds spice to life.

BERTRAND TAVERNIER : And ghosts, do you believe in them?

The old man props himself up on his pillows and prepares to tell us a story. He looks at us first, one after the other, with his lone blue eye.

FORD : Once in Ireland, I spent the night at the home of an old uncle of mine who had a chateau. He gave me his father's room, who had passed away long ago, an old friend of my father's. That room had a pretty bad reputation. During the night, I was woken up by a noise. I opened my eyes and saw an individual standing before me. I was wearing old clothes and particularly a lace jabot. He stood before me without saying anything and soon I recognized the great uncle.

Q : *Weren't you scared?*
FORD : No, because I knew that he had come just to see what the son of his old friend looked like.

Never in our lives had we heard such a short ghost story.

In public, he seems not to remember anything about his films. "I've never seen them," he says, which is probably half true. Only half because he is capable all of a sudden to talk about certain details concerning *The Iron Horse,* and if someone hums an air while telling him that it is the music from *Fort Apache,* he stops suddenly.

FORD: No, it's not *Fort Apache,* it's *Yellow Ribbon.* That's a great song.

Q: *You put a lot of folk music in your films?*
FORD: As much as I can. I love songs. Besides, they have recently become very popular in the U.S.A. with the new singers.

Now, he is more outgoing because he feels that we aren't there to dissect him, but to chat between friends on a voyage, and he even consents to talk to us about his films.

FORD: The films that I prefer are *The Sun Shines Bright,* whose main character is very close to me, and *Young Mr. Lincoln.* I am also very proud of *The Long Voyage Home, How Green Was My Valley, Drums Along the Mohawk, She Wore a Yellow Ribbon, Cheyenne Autumn.* I adore *Le Sergent Noir* (*Sergeant Rutledge,* he pronounces the title in French). They didn't want to let me do that film because they said a film about a "nigger" wouldn't make any money and because it couldn't be distributed in the South. I got angry and I told them that they could at least have the decency to say "Negro" or "colored man" instead of "nigger," because most "niggers" were worth more than they were. I found that out when I debarked on Omaha Beach: there were dozens of bodies of blacks spread out on the sand. When I saw that, I understood that it was impossible not to consider them as full-fledged Americans. And you know the funniest? The film makes a lot more money now in the South. Not with the whites, of course, but in the black cinemas where it is shown all the time. I have been told that in congregations, in little auditoriums, people rent projectors to be able to see this film. They are so happy to see a hero of their own race. Not a good, nice black, but a real hero.

I also like *The Fugitive.* I find my work on that film remarkable, if I do say so myself. People say so much bad about it. But I think it's one of my best films. It's like *7 Women.* The American critics say terrible things about it. But I am very proud. It's a story about women only. Almost all bitches. It is a story of bitchery. But they hated it. They are all Communists, those critics, and plus they hate the cinema.

Q: *Which ones don't you like?*
FORD: Oh, I don't know. *Tobacco Road, The Plough and the Stars,* which was massacred. When I finished the film, they redid the editing and an assistant re-shot a quarter of the film. *Born Reckless,* that's not my type of story.

Q: *And* Steamboat 'Round the Bend?
FORD: It was a very good film, but Zanuck arrived at Fox and he didn't have the least sense of humor. He cut all the gags out of the film. The two others that I shot with Will Rogers are better, especially *Judge Priest*, which is a success and very funny. That's a good film. It was the same character as in *The Sun Shines Bright. Air Mail,* that's good too. It's in that film that we improvised a character during the shooting. There was an actor named Slim Summerville, who hadn't made a film for a long time. He couldn't find work. Since actors have to eat from time to time, I took him with me and we added a character who didn't exist in the scenario.

Q: *Do you like comic scenes a lot?*
FORD: Yes. I am a director of comedies who makes sad films. I don't like happy endings. I like when they are melancholic.

Q: She Wore a Yellow Ribbon *is a sad film?*
FORD: Yes. It's a beautiful film. It was the one that the General MacArthur preferred. He saw it once a month. The last time I saw it, it was with him. And you know, in his speeches, he cited phrases from the dialogue or took pieces of John Wayne's final speech ("Old Soldiers never die"). Visually, I wanted to find the colors of Remington's paintings; and I had to fight with the chief cameraman who sent me written notes, affirming that he was in complete disagreement with my directives. During the shooting of the storm scene, he declared a few times that there wouldn't be anything on the negative. He got an Oscar for the film.

Q: *And* The Man Who Shot Liberty Valence?
FORD: It was a story full of pathos and tragedy. I had to fight for seven months to impose it. The banks didn't want it; besides nowadays nobody reads scenarios.

Q: *Did you really collaborate on* Hondo?
FORD: Yes, I filmed the exterior scenes and action scenes in the desert. I don't know how many exactly. Ten days at least. I did everything that happens in the desert. But I didn't do the indoor scenes. You know, I have often shot scenes in other films. I shot a film with Gary Cooper that way, I don't remember the title anymore. He had a small role. And I also did the difficult, spectacular scenes in *Marco Polo.*

Q: *And* Young Cassidy?
FORD: I shot for two days. The scenes with Julie Christie. I saw the film. They changed the end. Mine was much better, more violent.

Q: *Did you know Sean O'Casey?*
FORD: No. I never met him, but I like his theater. He was a rebel.

Q: *You collaborated on* The Brave and the Beautiful?
FORD: Oh! Yes, I remember that film. I don't remember the name of the director. Only his first name: Budd. I felt that young one had something, he was gifted. What was his name? Ah! Boetticher, Budd Boetticher. He had some trouble with the studio he worked for, so I helped him.

Q: *What profession would you have chosen if you hadn't been a filmmaker?*
FORD: Marine. Besides, I am a "matelot" (in French). That is why I like the nickname that the Navajo Indians have me: Natani Nez, which means Tall Soldier, Great Soldier. I am not a soldier, but a sailor. . . .

I am a man from the North. I was born in Maine, one of the first states to have abolished segregation. I hate the spirit of the South and I can't talk about it. . . . When I got married, my wife, who came from the South, brought her black nanny with her. We didn't need her. I didn't want to send her South because over there they don't know how to treat Blacks. So we bought her a house near us. It's a nice house. She is happy. She lives there now with her whole family. . . .

It is our last dinner with him. The atmosphere is really relaxed.

FORD: I don't understand the French. They spend hours in front of their menu as if it was a very serious subject. As long as I have confidence in the chef, I find that all the choices are equal!

He teases us, he is in good spirits. He orders his oeuf cocotte. He drinks his beer, some B and B (Benedictine and Brandy), wine too, but he assures us that wine is water, that it has nothing to do with alcohol. And on this subject he informs us that the Irish have the best wine in the world because there is an illicit traffic between France and Ireland: fishing boats import French wine to Ireland and return to France filled with Irish wool. Ford is enchanted. He is having fun and can tell stories between friends. He is on his own territory. He even sings old Irish songs, inviting us to sing with him.

And here, Ford talks to us of himself.

FORD: My childhood profoundly marked me. My father was very often homesick and wanted to return to Ireland. Since he lived in Maine, it was very easy. All he had to do was take the boat. And since I was the youngest, he took me with him. So, I spent my childhood between Ireland and America. I went to school in Ireland, and I left again for America. Until twelve, I didn't have a real home.

But it is beginning to get late. Ford isn't so young, he is tired, we accompany him to his room. I remain in the salon. His good mood is gone. I hear him repeat a few times like a wounded animal:

"It's over. They won't let me make any more films."

I'm eager for him to fall asleep. I don't want to hear that sentence anymore. But he repeats it again and again.

"They won't let me make any more films."

Notes of a Press Attaché: John Ford in Paris

BERTRAND TAVERNIER/1966

LIKE ALL WHO MET him, I sat down with his filmography in hand and asked him myriad questions, telling myself that all those people who had tried the same tack didn't know his films well and hadn't known how to speak to him about them. Well, it was a total flop. So I had to be content with listening and watching. And I tried to become his friend during the days we spent together.

It is not difficult to become his friend. Pierre Rissient, Jacques Ita, and I had been with him for a few minutes when he asked us to call him Jack, not "Mr. Ford." After an hour's time the ice was broken and we understood. We understood why well-known actors, upon getting a mere telegram from him, were willing to drop a job and travel long hours just to record a commentary or even simply visit him. We understood why some people became attached to him after meeting him for just a few minutes. And professionally, we understood how he was able to give some scenes so much warmth, to extract so much emotion from some performers.

Everything about John Ford commands respect. There was no softness in him, but instead a conquering, irresistible warmth, which often hides behind aggressiveness, and a quick, unpredictable humor, which he uses with diabolical deftness. The accusation of craftiness made by some soon collapsed. Clearly, Ford has never attempted to move or please by following the fashion or stacking the deck. . . . To be sure, Ford was old, very old, more than his

Originally printed in *Positif,* no. 82, March 1967. 7–22. Reprinted in *Film Comment,* vol. 30, no. 4. July/August 1994. 66 +. Reprinted by permission of the author.

age [seventy-one]. He still loved drinking but didn't tolerate alcohol as well as he used to, and he was terribly diminished by his wounds. At times, he was frightening, when his right side became paralyzed and prevented him from walking, or when his eyes became bloodshot. But his weaknesses were always physical—his mind remained clear. Very often, he surprised us with the swiftness with which he understood a tiny detail, with the way he was able to lead a conversation. We were not dealing with a mentally impaired old man but with a sick person who had been unconscionably allowed to travel alone.

According to witnesses we were able to question, in particular Romain Gary, who had known him for seventeen years, it was after completing *Cheyenne Autumn* ['64] that Ford aged ten years in two. The preparation of *Young Cassidy* ['65], the trip to Ireland, the location scouting probably didn't help any. Neither did the meetings with old friends, the parties, the pub-hopping. As a result, it was a seriously wounded man we had in front of us. A wounded man who, perhaps rightly, would not concede defeat. He fought off fatigue and sometimes won amazing victories, like the day we took him to watch Claude Chabrol shooting *Le Scandale* [U.S.: *The Champagne Murders*]. He seemed to live again, he looked five years younger. He was happy. . . .

It didn't take us long to realize that interviews bore him stiff. That was not what he had come for. Had we listened to him, they would all have been bunched together on the last day, and he would have spent [his visit] taking walks around Paris and meeting old friends. For press agents, the situation seemed disastrous. If fatigue and poor health, which made him unavailable for half of each day, were to be compounded with uncooperativeness, or at least visible boredom, the press coverage threatened to be limited. At that point we hit upon the idea of introducing the interviewers not as journalists but as friends of ours. This strategy yielded excellent results. As soon as Ford felt he could trust people, that he was not being spied upon, he started talking, telling stories, sometimes even giving information on his work. There was even one fantastic evening . . . but I am getting ahead of myself.

Otherwise, his dealings with journalists followed a kind of ritual. The same questions and answers kept recurring.

"Why have you made so many Westerns?"

"For health reasons. Westerns are a chance to get away from Hollywood and the smog. You live in the open, sleep under a tent, eat from a chuck wagon, barbecue your meat. It's great fun. At night, you get together and sing songs."

"Why did you become a film director?"

"I was hungry."

"What do you think is most characteristic of Hollywood?"

"The incredible number of churches. There are more than in any other town in the world, and what's more, they are full."

"What do you think of the remake of *Stagecoach*?"

"It's lousy. That sonofabitch Martin Rackin [the producer] had a dumb idea. I saw the movie and I think it's terrible. If I say so myself, I had done a couple of nice things [in the 1939 version] and they were new at the time, too. Why try to do it again?"

"Do you go to the movies?"

"No, never. Because you can't smoke."

Of course, we occasionally had to give up our stratagem. We were a little scared when it was the turn of Samuel Lachize, the film critic for *L'Humanite* [the French Communist Party's official daily paper]. Ford had asked a number of times if people might not shout "Yankee go home!" at him, and he had ranted against the Communists, in typical American fashion. Nevertheless, we introduced Lachize as a Communist critic. Ford didn't bat an eye: "Let him come in. I don't mind talking with a Communist . . . I'm a liberal."

Now, to our amazement, the interview went without a hitch. The two men immediately took to each other, and Ford didn't try to dodge the questions. He had them repeated to him, and answered at length, which was most unusual. He got angry only once, when Lachize told him that some people detected (wrongly, Lachize added) some racist aspects in his work:

"The people who say such things are crazy. I am a Northerner, I hate segregation, and I gave jobs to hundreds of Negroes at the same salary the whites were paid. I had production companies hire poverty-stricken Indians and pay them the highest Hollywood salaries for extras. Me, a racist? My best friends are black: Woody Strode, and a caretaker who has worked for me for thirty years. I even made *Sergeant Rutledge,* about a character who was not just a nice black guy but someone nobler than anybody else in the picture. They wouldn't let me make that picture because they said that a movie about a 'nigger' wouldn't make any money and couldn't be exhibited in the South. I got angry and told them they could at least have the decency to say 'Negro' or 'colored man,' because most of those 'niggers' were worth better than they. When I landed at Omaha Beach, there were scores of black bodies lying in the sand. Then I realized that it was impossible not to consider them full-fledged American citizens."

Ford returned to the subject several times and we had a hard time calming him down. He even mentioned the treatment of the Jews in the U.S.S.R. That was the only time he made a critical reference to his interviewer's ideology. His tone remained relaxed, but he had been stung. Suddenly, he called out to me, with his booming voice, asking for his rosary. He then handed it to Lachize, saying, "Take this, it's a gift. Come join our group." Lachize was dumbfounded. Ford took the rosary back. "I'll pray for you at Notre-Dame," he said as they parted. . . .

One evening he talked at length about his youth, about how he met his wife: "She had a higher rank than I did. I was a sergeant and she was a lieutenant in the nurses. Robert E. Lee and George Washington were among her ancestors—it was a great family—yet when she married this penniless Irish kid, they didn't object. And they're still not complaining about the marriage."

He also talked about the war, about how he had repulsed an Italian attack: "I was in command of a flotilla of landing barges, sailing in Indian file. Only the first and last ones were equipped with weapons. Suddenly, Italian planes appeared. We were in a tough spot. So I ordered top and rear boat to fire. At the first shell, the Italians vanished. They must have thought they were dealing with a new kind of warship, heavily armed, and they wouldn't come near."

He decided to discuss religion and declared himself anticlerical: "I hate preaching, but what I hate most is Irish priests. Besides, I select my priests the way I cast my pictures. I hate sanctimoniousness."

"What are your political opinions?"

"I am a liberal Democrat. And above all I am a rebel."

"Which presidents do you admire most?"

"Lincoln, Roosevelt, and John Kennedy. I loved Kennedy. He was a fantastic man, humorous, intelligent, generous. His assassination was a terrible blow to America. Despite what some have said, the Communists, the Russians are not behind his death. Oswald was a wretched fool who caused the country immense harm, what with Johnson being such a despicable man. He is a murderer."

"What about Bobby Kennedy?"

"He's far from being as good as John. He is an ambitious go-getter. Do you know that Kennedy's father was responsible for my making *The Informer* [at RKO]? . . . I didn't vote in the last election—Goldwater didn't have a serious platform and I hated Johnson."

"What do you think of organizations like the American Legion?"

"When they want to influence the way people vote, they become awful. One shouldn't allow such paramilitary outfits to meddle with politics. I hate people who want to tell you what to do."

This was practically the last time Ford discussed politics during his stay. There was one mystery, however, that we wanted to clarify:

"Is it true that you were one of the first to protest against McCarthyism?"

"Yes. I don't like Communists, but I can't stand people being persecuted or deprived of their freedom. I protested measures taken against directors or writers who were suspected [of Communism]. I was the first one to do so."

And of course Ford spoke of the West and Westerns:

"I knew Wyatt Earp. I heard the story of the O.K. Corral from him. I was my brother [Francis]'s assistant director and we made Westerns. The extras were real cowboys, actual friends of Earp's. He often came around to see them, and so I had a chance to speak to him. He was very tall, a man of few words, remarkably calm. He wasn't a good marksman, but he was very bold and so he would come very, very close to his opponent before shooting. This is the way it happens in my picture [*My Darling Clementine*, '46]. No one was fast on the draw in the West—that's a gimmick for fancy television cowboys. You pulled your gun and walked toward your enemy; you let him shoot first, then you tried to aim better than he had. Look at *Stagecoach* and *My Darling Clementine*. As for Doc Holliday, all he had in mind was to get himself killed. He looked for fights so that he could get shot."

"Do all your Westerns have a historical basis?"

"They do. *Fort Apache* is a variation on Custer's Last Stand. We changed the Indian tribes and the location. Fonda liked the part very much. In the military he had met many colonels, and he was himself given the rank of colonel at the end of the war. All he had to do was spend a few weeks in the West to get the feel of the country.

"*Liberty Valance* [*The Man Who Shot Liberty Valance*, '62] was based on historical fact, too. It was a fine story. I fought to make it."

"The theme of the family is very important to you. Why?"

"You have a mother, don't you?"

"Who are your favorite directors?"

"Leo McCarey—I love *Make Way for Tomorrow.* Frank Capra. And a whole bunch of other people, like Raoul Walsh, who's a fellow a little like me, except that he is handsomer and more of a ladies' man; one of his pictures, *The Honor System,* had impressed me a lot. Tay Garnett, Henry King. I like Sammy Fuller, too; he puts a little too much violence in his films, but unlike many others he doesn't do it for base commercial reasons—he is an upright, honest guy. I don't like John Huston, he is a phony."

That same evening ended on quite a moving note. Ford had just talked about his family, his son, his daughter, who was married to [actor/singer] Ken Curtis. When asked about Curtis's singing voice, he said: "Yes, he has a nice singing voice, except for the day I punched his face because he beat my daughter. It's hard to sing without teeth."

Then, after a couple of similar stories, Ford started talking to us about folk music and singing old Irish songs. One of them told of [French] General Hoche's crossing [in 1798], his failed landing, and the hopes it aroused among Irish insurgents. We found that Ford knew all the songs heard in his films. He corrected some of our mistakes: "There's a girl who sings all those old songs wonderfully, Connie Towers, Constance Towers [lead actress in *The Horse Soldiers,* '59, and *Sergeant Rutledge,* '60]. No one knows more old tunes than she does. Try to find her records."

After several songs, he went to bed, and it was then that he said, or rather kept repeating: "I can do whatever I want now because I'll never make another picture. They won't let me make one. They won't let me do another picture."

These words created dismay among us. He repeated them again and again, as though they were a statement of unavoidable fact. This haunting thought came up in many interviews. "I am a tough old retired director," he often said.

"Retired?"

"Well, half-retired. I'm waiting for someone to give me the go-ahead. I'm studying an offer from Samuel Goldwyn Jr. I want to make only a picture I like. I turned down many projects that I didn't approve of morally. Today, in the United States, directors film disgusting stories, and they don't even know how to shoot them. The French are much more gifted and more intelligent. I would like to make a picture on the American Revolution, although it's a taboo subject."

"You're mostly interested in stories set in the past?"

"Why do you say that? It's not true. I'm only interested in good stories. I don't ask myself if they're set in the past or not. And then, do you think the history of today's America is fun? I love to study the history of countries and races."

. . . Once in a while, we managed to glean a bit of information:

"In *The Wings of Eagles* ['57], Ward Bond plays me. . . . Republic was the studio where I had the most freedom. I did everything the way I wanted. . . . Black-and-white photography is much better than color. It's much more difficult to do fine photography in black and white. My finest color picture is *She Wore a Yellow Ribbon* ['49]. . . . Maureen O'Hara is one of the actresses I most dislike. Everybody thought I was her lover. Actually I hated her and she hated me, but she was right for the parts. I liked Joanne Dru [*She Wore a Yellow Ribbon* and *Wagon Master,* '50] and Elizabeth Allen [*Donovan's Reef,* '63; *Cheyenne Autumn,* '64]."

Ford had difficulty understanding why one should want to reissue his old films. One title prompted the following comment: "Ah, *Wagon Master*— that's the purest, most simple Western I made. The British love it. They made me come to Oxford or Cambridge to talk about it. Can you imagine me lecturing?"

"Do you dislike speaking about your films?"

"No, I don't. I just don't remember them. It's so far away. And then, the title often changed between shooting and the picture's release. Peter Bogdanovich came to my house to do a big interview for television. We're not progressing very fast, because he asks me about a picture and I tell him I didn't do it, then it turns out that the title had been changed."

"Your first big picture was *The Iron Horse* ['24]."

"It became big only by accident. We had started doing an ordinary picture, and then we got snowbound. We had nothing else to do, so we shot film and gradually the story developed. Many things happened, births, deaths, marriages, all of it in frigid weather. There was only one sunny day, and what we shot that day couldn't be used; those shots had to be done again in bad weather. It was an extraordinary experience. Fortunately, Union Pacific came to rescue us."

When Ford was told that I wanted to become a film director, he took me aside and started giving me advice:

"Careful, not too many camera moves. All the young kids who are starting out want to do crazy things with the camera. It's useless. The simplest continuity is the most efficient: a shot, then a reverse angle. You must spend more time with the actors and the dialogue than with the camera. Anybody can think up a difficult camera move, but very few people manage to retain the same feeling between a long shot and a closeup, to keep up the quality of emotion."

"Have you ever used a crane?"

"Never. It's awful. When I am asked why I hardly ever move the camera, I answer that the actors are better paid than the stagehands and grips, so it's normal that they should work and move about a little more. You should never use technical gimmicks to create emotion."

Elia Kazan has told me that it is precisely this quality he loves in Ford's films: "He was the first to dare use very lengthy long takes, going against Hollywood rules. He wouldn't cut to a closer shot. No one has been able to generate as much emotion as Ford does in long shots; watch *The Grapes of Wrath* and *Young Mr. Lincoln* ['39]."

"It's odd," Ford says, "I have a friend, his name is Elia Kazan, who often comes to see me. He tells me that before starting a picture he screens a lot of mine several times. I think this method is dumb. Yet he's a fine fellow, very intelligent. He must not be a great director."

The ten days or so that I spent working with John Ford in Paris were one of the sources of inspiration for *Round Midnight* ('86). All those days and nights spent keeping him from drinking, hiding glasses under couches, under the bed, trying to protect him, I relived while writing that film, and especially while shooting it with Dexter Gordon.

It was Pierre Rissient who got the first shock, when he met Ford at the airport. Ford came off the plane completely smashed, unable to stand up, so that he had to be put in a wheelchair. We had to deal with an invalid.

We fought hard, tirelessly taking turns at his bedside, drinking half the drinks he ordered. That was not enough, unfortunately. In a recent article, Irish journalist Peter Lennon recalled that he gave up trying to arouse Ford from his alcohol-induced stupor and settled for interviewing me instead. However, we did manage to keep him clear-minded for a few hours a day. In the worst moments, we kept him from firing the captain of his yacht, against whom he would fly into sudden fits of anger. He then would decide to call him on the phone to dismiss him. We had a chance to intervene in some of these insane conversations, worthy of W. C. Fields's delirious outbursts. . . .

[POSTSCRIPT] I saw Ford again a few years later when Pierre Rissient had him come to France in an effort to set up a production of *Boule de Suif.* He was more sober and looked in better shape. It was then that Leslie Caron rejected the title role in this project, arguing that Ford was not as modern a director as Nanni Loy because he never moved the camera, while Loy used traveling shots. That's the film expertise of actresses for you.

Ford on Ford 2

AXEL MADSEN/1967

FORD IS IN BED, saying he has had a rough day.

AXEL MADSEN: *Are you preparing a film?*
JOHN FORD: I decided to retire. I said, "What the hell, at my age," I've worked hard enough and I can go fishing. But since I decided to retire, I've never worked so much. I've had more scripts to read, people kept sending them, all dirty, filthy, so I said, "Oh, to hell with it." You as a Protestant can do them!

M: *Last year, you mentioned a film you might do in Alaska, a Navy story.*
F: I doubt we'll make it. I could get the cooperation of the Navy as an ex-Admiral, but there's also the Pentagon. I'd have to go not to Alaska but almost to the North Pole, and they haven't enough ships.

M: *So are you thinking of teaching at UCLA, the way Josef von Sternberg had been doing?*
F: No, I couldn't teach them how to make dirty pictures. I think I'll take a vacation, and then hope to make a movie.

Interviewed April 4, 1967. © Axel Madsen. A version of this interview was published in *John Ford: En Dokumentation*, ed. Per Colum. Danish Film Museum, 1968. The Danish portions of the original transcript of the interview were translated by Jan Lumholdt, who preserved Ford's original English. Printed by permission of the author.

M : *Which one?*

F : It's called *April Morning,* from a historical novel by Howard Fast. It wasn't a best seller but it was very popular. It's a simple family story, a beautiful, lovely story that ends with the battle of Lexington. It's not a battle story per se, like a Yugoslavian picture with thousands of horsemen. It's not a story with hundreds of people, just a few.

I talked to the French about this movie, and they were enthused. After all, the French did win the Revolutionary War for us. There were four French regiments at the battle of Yorktown. I'm considering doing a picture in France, a very interesting one. It's a great French classic, a short story, and don't ask me the name of it. I won't tell you because the producer has forgot to register the title.

M : *I thought producers were smart.*

F : Did you? (Laughter.)

M : *Do you prefer to make films about exceptional people?*

F : I can't answer that. I have no fixed principle. I mean, if a good story comes along, I'll do it regardless. My best pictures are made about little people, pictures you've never seen. The one I'm most proud of is *The Sun Shines Bright.*

M : *What about your latest pictures,* The Man Who Shot Liberty Valance *and* 7 Women?

F : They're not my favorites. I prefer little pictures that cost less than half a million dollars. *Young Mr. Lincoln* is one of my favorites.

M : *We were impressed by* Seven Women. *The screenplay and casting are very good, and you constantly move between the moral and social significance.*

F : Never mind about *Seven Women.* You asked me what the best pictures were. I said *The Sun Shines Bright* and *Young Mr. Lincoln,* and a picture I made in Ireland called *Three Leaves of a Shamrock,* which was a trilogy, three very simple, beautiful stories. The studio didn't like it. No stars, sex, or violence.

M : *In many of your pictures there is a dance, a rare moment when your people, in a difficult period of their lives, relax. Can you explain?*

F :   A short dance is always good, some of our American folk dances are interesting. In *The Long Voyage Home,* it was a very natural thing to do when men had been for months at sea.

M :   *Did you ever see the remake of* Stagecoach?
F :   I looked at a quarter of it with another director, William Wellman, and he said, "Let's go to the can." So we both went and threw up and left the theatre. (Laughter.) He was a helluva guy. He was with the Lafayette Escadrille in 1918. He shed a little blood for France, as I did.

M :   *Do you remember* Four Men and a Prayer *that you made in 1938 with Loretta Young? You had a stairs scene that reminds everybody of* The Battleship Potemkin.
F :   I didn't want to do that picture, and I raised hell, but I had it under contract. I made it but I didn't see it. As for taking it from *Potemkin,* I never saw that one.

M :   *Were there many films that you didn't want to make?*
F :   Oh, Christ, a lot of them. But in those days you were under contract. Now we're all freelancers.

M :   *Do you know that John Wayne is going to make a picture about the Vietnam War?*
F :   Perhaps. I think he's having a little trouble with it.

M :   *Do you see each other frequently?*
F :   No, he lives miles and miles away down in Newport. We talk on the phone.

M :   *Were the parts he played in movies often changed specifically to suit him?*
F :   I couldn't answer that. He sort of plays himself. He'd been my second assistant prop man, and I put him in *Stagecoach.* Walter Wanger didn't mind. The budget was so low we made it in three weeks, what the hell. Westerns were taboo in those days. After *Stagecoach,* everybody started doing them.

M :   Stagecoach *is kind of a milestone in the evolution of the Western. Were you conscious of that when you made it?*

F : Of course not. I liked that the story was a bit unusual. A lot of action, good characters. Now *How the West Was Won* had a big budget, but it was not particularly successful here because of American youth. The teenagers can't understand it. To them an American Indian is the somebody to be killed, he is the enemy. In my pictures, the Indians are the heroes. So that one wasn't successful, but I like it.

M : *And you like Monument Valley.*
F : That's why I do Westerns occasionally. It's not that I'm particularily fond of Westerns, but I like to get out in the open spaces. I like to get away from *this* space, away from the smog.

M : *When you originally brought films to show the Indians, how did they react?*
F : They were amazed. They'd never seen a picture before, and they didn't recognize themselves. Every night we'd show one. No emotion, but they obviously liked them because they'd gather and say, "Another picture tonight."

M : *How were they to work as actors?*
F : Great. The Navajos are the best riders in the world. They are good actors, much simpler to work with than a similar group of white extras.

M : *Talk about your cinematographers.*
F : Gregg Toland and Joe August were the best two cameramen we had, but they're all good now, all alike. I'm myself the best cameraman in the world, and I'm a very modest person. No, I'm kidding, but I'm a very good cameraman.

M : *The big studio bosses in the early days? Weren't they rather easy to get along with, once they had given their OK?*
F : They were very easy. In those days, we had no budgets. We went out and made a picture. When we started out on *The Iron Horse,* a blizzard came up and it lasted for two days. I said, "Hell, let's start anyway." We were there for three or four weeks, and finally the boss, Sol Wurtzel, came up and said, "Jesus, we've got a big picture here. Take all the time you need."

M : *Did you know John Steinbeck? What did he think of the shooting of* The Grapes of Wrath?

F :   I don't think John has ever been to a studio. He never bothered to come and see. The only author I ever knew who showed any enthusiasm about a picture was Eugene O'Neill for *The Long Voyage Home.* Once a month in the evening they'd set a screening room aside and he'd come in and look at his picture. They'd give him a huge tray so he could smoke his cigarettes. He'd sit there alone, or sometimes he brought his wife, sometimes a friend. He's the only author who liked what I did with his work, which is a great compliment since, after all, O'Neill is a great playwright.

M :   *Did you enjoy making films more in the old days?*
F :   Oh, yes. Now it's a task, too many people at the top. To use a paraphrase: never have so few been directed by so many from so far away. You know?

M :   *Aren't there others in your family who want to make movies, your grandsons?*
F :   They're in Vietnam.

Burt Kennedy Interviews John Ford

BURT KENNEDY/1968

FORD WAS INTERVIEWED BY BURT Kennedy, who has demon-
strated his facility with the Western with such films as *Mail Order Bride, The
Rounders, Return of the Seven, Welcome to Hard Times, The War Wagon, The
Train Robbers.*

KENNEDY: *I never saw* The Iron Horse.
FORD: You weren't even born when I made that one.

KENNEDY: *I know. I have heard that* The Iron Horse *was your favorite picture.
Is that true?*
FORD: No. "The next one" is my favorite picture. Well, maybe there's one
that I love to look at again and again. That's *The Sun Shines Bright,* a Judge
Priest story by Irvin S. Cobb, who was a pretty damn good writer. I had
Charles Winninger in that one and he was excellent. That's really my fa-
vorite.

The only trouble was that when I left the studio, old man [Herbert] Yates
didn't know what to do with it. The picture had comedy, drama, pathos, but
he didn't understand it. His kind of picture had to have plenty of sex or
violence. Yates fooled around with it after I left the studio and almost ruined
it.

Originally printed in *Action,* vol. 3, no. 5. September/October 1968. Reprinted in *Directors in
Action,* ed. Bob Thomas. Indianapolis, 1973. 133–39. Reprinted by permission of the Directors
Guild of America.

KENNEDY: The Quiet Man—*That was a wonderful picture.*

FORD: Yes. I like that one. There again I had trouble with Yates. He kept complaining, "It's all green. Don't they have any browns or blacks in Ireland? Why does it have to be all green?" I had a lot of fun with old Herb on that one. He wanted to call it *The Prize Fighter and the Colleen.* I felt that was an awful title because it tipped the story that Duke [Wayne] was a boxer. Well, Yates said that he had received lots of letters from exhibitors who told him that they preferred his title to *The Quiet Man.* I asked to look at the letters, and he showed them to me. "What a strange coincidence!" I told him. "All these letters have the same date and they say the same thing." Obviously he had sent out a letter that was practically mimeographed and asked the theater men to write in letters. And they did. But I still wouldn't go with his title.

KENNEDY: *I've made practically all Westerns, and I keep hearing the remark, "Why don't you change the mold?" Has that ever happened to you?*

FORD: No one has ever told me what kind of picture to make. When [Merian] Cooper and I were starting our own company, I made four or five Westerns in order to make some money. They were potboilers, but they served a purpose.

KENNEDY: *I love to make Westerns.*

FORD: So do I. It's a great life—just like a paid vacation. I love to make Westerns. If I had my choice, that's all I would make.

KENNEDY: *Have you seen any of these Spanish or Italian Westerns?*

FORD: You're kidding!

KENNEDY: *No, they have them, and a few have been popular.*

FORD: What are they like?

KENNEDY: *No story, no scenes. Just killing—fifty or sixty killings per picture. . . . How do you prepare for a picture?*

FORD: Well, you ask yourself a few questions: What are you going to say? What is your format? Right now I'm wrestling with a story about the OSS. I made a promise to Wild Bill Donovan on his death bed that I would make an OSS picture, so I've got to do it. Right now I'm wading through piles of reports and histories and trying to break it down into some kind of a format. I'm suffering from a wealth of material. But you try to get a format for each picture. For instance, on *She Wore a Yellow Ribbon* I tried to make it as Remington as possible, though it didn't quite come out that way. On another picture I might try to make it as if it were seen by Charlie Russell.

KENNEDY: *I was just down in Sedona [Arizona] shooting a picture, and I liked that location.*
FORD: Yes, Sedona is okay, but it's too small, too confined. If I'm going on location, I'd rather go farther, to some big place like Monument Valley.

KENNEDY: *Did you ever have any trouble getting the studios to let you go to the right places?*
FORD: No.

KENNEDY: *We're always bucking to go to a good location, but the studio always wants you to shoot it on the back lot.*
FORD: I never had that. I wouldn't make a Western on the back lot. They could get somebody else.

KENNEDY: *Did you ever have any problems with big-money actors?*
FORD: No, I never ran into that problem.

KENNEDY: *Well, you know, the actors now have their own companies.*
FORD: No, I never had that. I wouldn't work with an actor's company. Oh, I did some pictures with Duke when he had his Batjac, but I wasn't working for him. I never had any trouble with actors; if anybody kicked up a fuss, I'd say, "Okay, we'll get somebody else."

KENNEDY: *What do you think of the various wide-screen processes?*
FORD: I still like the conventional-sized screen.

KENNEDY: *So do I. I think the 1.85 ratio is the best.*
FORD: You're right. It still has height and you can get composition. It's so hard to get good composition in a wide screen. I like to see the people and if you shoot them in a wide screen, you're left with a lot of real estate on either side.

KENNEDY: *I like to tell a small story against a big background. It seems to me that you did that in* The Searchers.
FORD: Yes, and that was in the ordinary-size screen. But then, I still like to work in black and white.

KENNEDY: *Why?*
FORD: You like spinach? It's all a matter of taste. But anybody can shoot color; you can get a guy out of the street and he can shoot a picture in color. But it takes a real artist to do a black-and-white picture.

KENNEDY: *Speaking of artists, I had Bert Glennon as cameraman on one of my first pictures. He kept telling me to look through the camera, and finally I told him, "I don't have to; I know it's going to be a good shot." Bert said, "Yes, but you won't have me every time on a picture."*
FORD: Yes, Bert was a god-damn good cameraman. It's a good idea to get a cameraman you know well and can trust.

KENNEDY: *I use the same actors in pictures over and over again.*
FORD: Yes. I did that, too. It's good to have actors you can trust, ones who will know their lines and be there.

KENNEDY: *I fight to get good actors in small parts. I find you not only get a better performance, but you save time, because they know their job.*
FORD: That's a good idea. It pays to get good actors. I remember in *The Searchers* I had a scene where all an actor had to do was go through the door and take his suspenders off. I did the scene thirty-five times, and the actor still didn't do it right. I couldn't figure out what was wrong. Finally I asked him, "Did you read the script?" He said he didn't. I said, "For Crissake, don't you realize what you're doing? You're going to bed and leaving your wife outside with Duke Wayne." The actor said, "Christ I didn't know that. Most of us who play small bits never read the script. We just come in, find out what the director wants, do the part and leave." I shot the scene one more time, and the actor got it right in the first take.

KENNEDY: *Many times the studios will send actors only the few pages that they're involved in. That's a mistake.*

FORD: Of course it is. Every actor is better if he knows what the hell the story is about. I always give everybody a script and we have a reading with the whole cast the day before the picture starts. I want to let all of them know what they're doing.

KENNEDY: *I find myself spending more time in the cutting room with the cutter after the picture is over, and I won't let anybody see the picture until I've made my final cut. I find if I stay in the cutting room, then the picture doesn't become the work of a committee.*
FORD: You're right. You can't make pictures by committees. At one studio I had all the executives coming to the rushes, including the lawyers, and they started giving me lots of advice. I stopped that. I never let the cast see the rushes. I did that once, and the next day every character in the picture changed. One of the actresses said, "Oh, I look so old. Can't you put in a fade-back where I look young and beautiful?" After that I wouldn't let any actors see the rushes.

KENNEDY: *How much preparation do you do the night before shooting?*
FORD: None. I come home at six o'clock in the evening and I'm through. I find it much better to get there in the morning for a cup of coffee and sit around and talk to the actors about what they're going to do that day. I figure I work hard all day and when I come home I deserve a rest. Nobody discusses pictures in the house. My wife never sees pictures; she only goes out at night to Anaheim to see the Angels play. Do you work at home at night?

KENNEDY: *No, no. I used to, but I've found that I got locked in and couldn't change my thinking when I got to the set and found things were not the same as I had expected.*
FORD: Yes, you can walk into a set and find it altogether different. But if you have preconceived notions, you may lose the atmosphere entirely.

KENNEDY: *One thing I do—I'm awfully aware of wardrobe. I always see the fittings of any of the characters in the picture.*
FORD: We all do, don't we?

KENNEDY: *No, I don't think so.*
FORD: I guess you're right. I've seen some pictures that made me say, "Why in God's name did the director ever let the star wear that costume?" Or "Why did that woman wear such a dress?"

KENNEDY: *Is it true that you "cut in the camera?"*

FORD: Yes, that's right. I don't give 'em a lot of film to play with. In fact, Eastman used to complain that I exposed so little film. But I did cut in the camera. When I take a scene, I figure that's the only shot there is. Otherwise, if you give them a lot of film, when you leave the lot the committee takes over. They're all picture makers; they know exactly how to put a picture together and they start juggling scenes around and taking out this and putting in that. They can't do it with my pictures. I cut in the camera and that's it. There's not a lot of film left on the floor when I've finished.

KENNEDY: *I'm the same way, too. I've never lost a sequence in a picture. I think my cut of* War Wagon *was only eighteen seconds longer than the final release—the studio took out a scene with Kirk Douglas in his bare fanny. They don't have much film to play with when I'm finished either.*

FORD: You know, I think you've been copying me, Burt.

KENNEDY: *You know, you're absolutely right.*

John Ford

DOCUMENTARY FILM GROUP/1968

In APRIL 1968, JOHN Ford visited the University of Chicago at the invitation of the student Documentary Film Group. Mr. Ford participated in a question-and-answer session after a screening of a 16mm version of *The Long Voyage Home,* which seemingly had been "edited" for home viewing.

FORD: A disgrace, a rotten blasted shame. I'm humiliated by this print. They've cut it up for television and in the process someone has lifted three connecting sequences bodily out of the film. What a crime! The people who watch this on television must think I'm out of my mind.

(Laughter from the audience.)

FORD: There's nothing funny about it. It's like having the best pages blotted out of your M.A. thesis. If it weren't for the good nuns present from my own religion, I'd say "Goddamned television!" (Smiles impishly.) But the good nuns are present, so I won't.

Q: *What got you to make* The Long Voyage Home?
FORD: The sea had always meant a great deal to me. I wanted to do a story about the sea, about ships, but every story I got, they always sneaked a girl

From *Focus,* no. 5. October 1969. 3–4. Reprinted by permission of Doc Films, the University of Chicago.

aboard. It's true! I was talking to Eugene O'Neill (he was a very dear friend of mine) about it, and he said, "Jack, you must have seen my trilogy, *The Long Voyage Home.*" And I said I had. So he suggested that the plays could be strung together to make a picture, and I said, "That's a wonderful idea." So we knocked it out. And what's more, Gene liked the film.

Q : *How did you get those special effects in* Hurricane?
FORD : Those were all studio sets.

Q : *How do you decide where to place the camera?*
FORD : Say I've got three people, what's the best way to photograph them? What's the best background? How shall I separate them? If it's an important scene, I may want to take individual closeups. Instinct, something can't be taught.

Q : *Did you feel that* The Grapes of Wrath *was consistent with your other films?*
FORD : Yes, very much so; it's the kind of story I *do* like. I like to work with people, characters; my whole method is to read a book or story, and I try to put on the screen what the author is trying to say. I was reared in poverty, so the picture appealed to me. I enjoyed making it very much. I know John Steinbeck very well and I talked it over with him and just tried to do it as it was. John liked it very much when it was finished.

Q : *Were the Bostonians in* Donovan's Reef *overdone?*
FORD : Oh, no. You can't overdo them.

Q : *Do you think film schools such as USC and UCLA are a good idea?*
FORD : I think film schools are a very good idea. You learn something; then it's not something completely new you're going into.

Q : *What other directors and pictures do you like?*
FORD : I just saw *A Man for All Seasons,* Freddie Zinneman sent it over. It was a great movie; Freddie's a very fine director.

Q : *What was your approach to working in color—in* 7 Women, *for instance.*
FORD : I tried to keep the film down to a monotone, to start, and later on, when the girl (Anne Bancroft) put on the kimono, I went into rather vivid

color for a sudden change. But the first part was pretty much in monotone. I kept it in browns, blacks, and whites, kept all the reds out of the thing.

Q : *Has your attitude toward the western changed in your career?*
F O R D :   No, still the same as ever. I never go to see a western and I'd never think of reading a western novel or story. I only make them to get away from the smog of Hollywood. . . . I'm just a hard-nosed working director.

Q : *There are no changes between* The Iron Horse *in 1924 and* The Man Who Shot Liberty Valance?
F O R D :   Ah, *Liberty Valance!* Yes. The man didn't kiss his horse and ride off into the sunset.

Ford in Person

MARK HAGGARD/1970

JOHN FORD HAS MADE two recent appearances at the University
of Southern California in Los Angeles, both times as the honoured guest of
USC's Alpha chapter of DKA, the national honorary cinema fraternity. In the
spring of 1969, DKA sponsored a thirty-film Ford retrospective and, in the
spring of 1970, a monumental, semester-long "History of the Western,"
which included five of Ford's best-loved films.

On both occasions, Ford was brief, colourful and candid, more often than
not revealing himself most fully between the lines. He doesn't like to talk
about films in an abstract, analytical fashion, but he is a born storyteller, and
there is nothing he would rather do than regale a few friends with stories
about the making of films and the actors and fellow craftsmen with whom
he has worked. . . .

On the first occasion, on a Saturday night in March of 1969, Ford was introduced to the audience by writer Peter Bogdanovich and the then-president
of DKA, Father Frank Frost, S.J., who was, fortunately, dressed in his clerical
collar.

Ford began: "Members of DKA—ladies and gentlemen—guests. . . ." Here
he paused for a moment, then turned to Frost and added, "Father . . ." and
the audience laughed. "Beg your pardon," he said, "I forgot all about you.
And with Saint Patrick's Day coming up." There was another laugh, and then
Ford turned back to the audience.

"First," he said, "as an Irishman, I've gotta wish you all, may the day be

From *Focus on Film 6.* Spring 1971. 31–37. Reprinted by permission of Tantivy Press.

clear and the road be clear before you. Monday is Saint Patrick's Day and tonight all the friendly sons of Saint Patrick"—he looked at his watch—"no, they're not getting unfriendly yet." [*Laughter*] "In about an hour, they'll start getting unfriendly and they'll be hitting each other over the heads with bottles . . .

"Well, you're probably used to these pedagogic, pedantic treatises on how to make a motion picture—the theme, the theory, and everything else. Well, I can't give you a talk on that, because I don't know how, I haven't got the mental capacity, the capability, for doing that. I couldn't read it, because"—he held his hand out in front of his face—"it'd have to stand out there some place, because I have split focus in this eye. As a matter of fact, I think I'm quite a guy for coming up here tonight. I've been in bed with a couple of cracked ribs all week, and I didn't want to disappoint you. You just saw—what were you looking at, what picture?"

"*The Searchers*," said Bogdanovich.

"Oh!" said Ford. "There's one thing that strikes me about *The Searchers*: this is really an almost all-out USC cast." [*Laughter*] "Oh, it is! That's not supposed to be a joke. There's Michael Morrison, whom you know better as John Wayne; Ward Bond; Jeffrey Hunter (he had his freshman year here); Jackie Williams, whom you won't know—he was a famous polo player here; Russ Saunders; oh, there's several others whose names slip me at the moment. But it's practically a USC cast."

Here Ford's voice became softer, and he said: "Of course, Ward has gone and left us, and Duke and I—Duke Wayne, I mean—this is something that has gone out of our lives. We were a great trio together. Ward was a—just a wonderful guy. . . .

"So I thought I'd tell you a couple of stories about incidents that happened on location. I don't think people tell you about those things. They get a dictionary and write a thesis and read that to you. . . .

"Ward Bond was a great big, ugly, wonderful guy. But he was a terrific snob. This was the greatest snob I have ever known. Now, I don't understand snobbery. Ward's father was a coal miner—which is a very honourable profession. (*My* father was a saloonkeeper—which is even more honourable)." [*Laughter*]

"But Ward was striving for better things. We were down—working down in Florida, and every night he broke up the card game, see, and he put on a white dinner coat with a red cummerbund and went out. I says: 'Where are you going?' and he says: 'Out with some society people.' So Wayne and I and Bob Montgomery, we had a cab waiting and we sneaked after him. We sneaked in and watched him, and there was Ward sitting at the head of the table, and he had ordered the wine, he was looking at the wine''—here Ford pantomimed Bond examining the wine bottle—''and he says: 'Hmm . . .' Now he didn't know anything about wine, I mean . . .'' [*Laughter*] '' 'Is that the best year you have? Do you have a . . . umm . . . '48?'—which happens to be one of the worst vintages ever made, you know—and he says: 'That'll be all right.' And he was very tight—he never bought anything for *us*—and here he was buying, and I says: 'Who are those people?' and he says, 'That fellow's the leading druggist in Dubuque, Iowa!' I says: 'Well, that's really society!' '' [*Laughter*]

"Duke and I were always spending most of our time thinking up tricks to play on Ward. If we spent half the time, just one quarter of the time, reading the script or trying to help the story, we'd have made better pictures. . . .

"Ward always wanted to be the leading man, and he was very jealous of Duke. They were the best of friends—all three of us were, the very best of friends—but he was always jealous of Duke, and he used to say: 'I should be playing that part, of course, you know that,' and I says: 'Yeah, sure you should, yeah.' '' [*Laughter*]

"But we would have more fun with him, and, as I say, we should have thought more about the picture and less about playing jokes on Ward. I suppose the 'Dear Mabel' joke is not in your time." Here Ford raised his voice to a falsetto and crooned: '' 'Oh, Mabel, dear, Mabel darling.' Anybody familiar with it? Hm? 'Mabel darling.' Well, we used to pull that one on—that goes back, I mean, my God, to the flood." [*Laughter*]

"Well, I'm going on location. We had to land DC-3s in. And we carefully picked out a very lush gal. She was really stacked. She was going to do a bit in the picture. (She was up there for legitimate purposes.) But we had her well schooled, and we carefully put her in the first plane, and the assistant got strict orders to get her in the first car and send her out to hide. And then Ward was in the second plane, see. And he got out there and did the usual kicking about his room—y'know, he wanted a southern exposure—he kicked about everything, didn't like his part, and I says: 'Well, fine, go home,' and he says: 'Oh, well, y'know, don't wanna do that . . .' '' [*Laughter*]

"The first night we sat down for dinner—we're all in Gouldings—and there were about ten of us at the table, and this girl came in, this''—and here

Ford sneaked a brief look at Father Frost—"with all due deference to Father—who I said was very well stacked—and she came in dressed as a waitress, and with an autograph book, and says: 'Mr. Bond, you are my favourite actor. I think you're just wonderful. Why do they have you playing these old parts?'

" 'Well', says Ward, pointing to me, 'ask him, ask him.' " [*Laughter*]

"And she says: 'I think you're just sweet. Would you like a steak? I've got one laid aside for you, a very special steak.'

" 'Yeah, a steak, honey. What's your name, dear?'

"She says: 'Mabel.'

" 'Oh, that's a beautiful name.' " Ford pantomimed Bond signing his autograph. " 'Dear Mabel!—with love, Ward.'

"And he looks at us with triumph, and the girl went off, and somebody says: 'Hey, what about *our* food?' and she says: 'I'll get it as soon as I serve Mr. Bond.'

"Well, this kept up for two days, and she was fussing around Ward, and Ward was preening himself, and he was really in great shape. And then she told him, she says: 'You know, my husband's working on the Atchison, Topeka, and Santa Fe, and he'll be in the day after tomorrow. It's too bad—I'm going to miss walking in the moonlight with you, darling.'

"And he says: 'Well, where do you live?'

"And she says: 'Well, you know that bunch of cabins—I'm on the end cabin, I'm all alone there.'

" 'Oh,' he says, 'how about me dropping in tonight?'

" 'Oh, I'd love that,' she says. 'Look, honey, bring a six-pack of beer and a watermelon.' " [*Guffaws*]

"He says: 'They have watermelons here, don't they?'

"And she says: 'Well, they don't serve the help and ah'm from the South, you know'—she's suddenly changed her accent—'and ah *love* watermelon.' And, anyway, they made this pact.

"Nine-thirty he appeared—a six-pack of beer, a watermelon under his arm—put the beer down and knocked. 'Mabel, dear? . . . Mabel?'

" 'Is that you, Ward?'

" 'Yes, darling.

" 'The door is open.'

"So he picks up the six-pack and goes in, and we're all inside with frontier-type pistols, and there's eight of us, and we went BANG! BANG! BANG! BANG! BANG!—anyway, Jesus—BANG! It was awful!" [*Uproarious laughter*]

"Well, Ward lit out of there—he made O. J. Simpson look like a tortoise. He dropped the six-pack, but he still carried the watermelon under his arm, and he sprinted out into the desert. I got the lead wrangler, I said: 'Mount up some horses and go out there and pick him up.' And we went BANG! BANG! BANG! BANG! until all six shots—so eight times six—ahem—I flunked mathematics" [*Laughter*] "What's that come to?

"Well, we pulled jokes like that on him, that's one I always remembered. And meanwhile, I mean, I don't want you to think I'm saying anything derogatory about Ward, God rest his soul—he was a wonderful guy. I miss him and Wayne misses him, and something has gone out of our lives. He's the godfather to my children and my grandchildren, and he's a very dear friend".

"Didn't he once play you in a picture?[1]" said Bogdanovich.

"I don't remember," said Ford quickly, looking at his watch again, causing another ripple of laughter. "Anyway, a lot of funny things happened on location. You try to take advantage of them and use them in the picture and sometimes they work out. *Now*—has anybody really got an in-ter-esting question that they might want to ask?" There was no immediate response, and Ford didn't wait for one. "God help us, no," he muttered. "Good!" he exclaimed, and began taking his mike off.

Before leaving, he paused to explain to the audience that he had asked DKA not to show *The Quiet Man* in the only available print, which was black-and-white, "because the colour is part of the dramatic structure of the story. In black-and-white, the scene does not go over."

In February of the following year, at the time of his seventy-fifth birthday, Ford paid another visit to USC. This time, as he entered the room, the audience serenaded him with a chorus of "Happy Birthday." He seemed pleased.

On this occasion, Ford was accompanied by Dick Amador, an old Navy comrade, and was introduced by Father Frost, who, since last year, had grown a beard. As Father Frost slipped the mike around his neck, Ford said: "Oh, we're going to get the last rites again, hm?"

He began by explaining that when Father Frost came to his house earlier, "I didn't recognise him—since he's turned hippy. But now I recognise him, in this light . . .

"Well, Father Frost, ladies and gentlemen"—he began chuckling—"I almost said: 'fellow alumni.' It's very funny. When I left—got kicked—I mean, when I left college . . ." He suddenly looked at Father Frost. "That's a story

which, despite your beard, it's too difficult to tell you—why I suddenly left
. . . well, let's not mention any names." [*Laughter*] "Now they want me to go
back, and they want to name their school of dramatic arts 'The John Ford
School of Dramatic Arts,' and I says: 'Hell, they kicked me out once, I wanta
stay kicked out.' " [*Laughter*] "I was gonna say, I almost said 'fellow alumni.'
Because I was an assistant director and when I left school there were many
gaps in my education . . ." Suddenly Ford stopped, noticing out of the corner
of his eye that someone had leaned over to whisper something to Father
Frost. "What were you whispering about, huh?" he said.

"He wanted you to talk about *Clementine* some time," said Father Frost.
"But he didn't want to interrupt."

"The movie," said Frost.

"You're not interested in why I almost called you 'fellow alumni'?" [*Enormous laughter*] "Well, anyway. . . . There were many gaps in my education,
and there're still many gaps in it. But the strange thing . . . I come from the
state of Maine, and for some reason they do not teach American history.
They have Greek, Egyptian, Roman, French, and English, but we were never
taught American history. So one day someone says to me: 'There's a fellow
here who's an associate professor at USC. He's a real ham at heart, and he
loves movies, and I wish you'd use him whenever you can, he's a nice fellow.
He teaches night school.' So I went up to this fellow and said: 'You teach
American history?' and he says: 'Yes.' And I says: 'Well, let's make a deal. I'll
use you as much as possible.'

And I went down there two, sometimes three nights a week—down to the
American history class. So I now know what the Gadsden Purchase is—I
never knew before. And so I settled the—what'd you want to know about
Clementine?" [*Laughter*]

"Before you talk about that,' said Father Frost, "I think the people in the
audience are probably wondering who the man on your right is."

"This is my executive officer, Chief Petty Officer Amador," said Ford. "We
were in the Navy together for twenty years, and he's just out now, he's done
his twenty years. And a very, very good man. When I became Admiral, I
wanted to promote him to Lieutenant Senior Grade—and he screamed. Because he'd get $80 a month *less* that way"—Ford chuckled—"than if he were
a Chief Petty Officer.

"About *Clementine*, the only story I know about it—Wyatt Earp moved
out here and lived some place beyond Pasadena, and his wife was a very

religious woman, and two or three times a year. . . . Can you hear me all right?"

"Yes," the audience answered.

"I can use my bridge voice, you know!" yelled Ford loudly. "Cause I have commanded ships!" [*Laughter*]. Resuming his normal tone, he continued: "And when she'd go away on these religious conventions, Wyatt would sneak into town and get drunk with my cowboys; Along about noon, they'd sneak away and come back about 1:15 swacked to the gills—all my cowboys *and* Wyatt—and I'd have to change the schedule around. And he told me the story of the fight at the O.K. Corral. And that was exactly the way it was done, except that Doc Holliday was not killed. Doc died of tuberculosis about eighteen months later. And that's about the only story I know about *Clementine*—except that the finish of the picture was not done by me. That isn't the way I wanted to finish it. However . . ."

"How did you want it?" someone asked.

"It was so long ago I've forgotten, but it wasn't that way at all. I think I wanted the girl to stay there and teach school, and I wanted Wyatt to stay there and become permanent marshal—which he did. And that was the true story. Instead of that, he had to ride away. But, uh . . .

"I've been in a terrible automobile crash, and I broke a rib and cracked three others, and my doctor forbade me to get out of bed and come down here. He says: 'Where are you going?' and I says: 'USC.' and he says: 'Oh, that's all right.' Y'see, he's a graduate of USC." [*Laughter*]

"So—ladies and gentlemen, that's about all I've got to say, and I thank you very much for this warm welcome."

"I'm sure there are many questions if you think you could answer a couple," said Father Frost.

Ford looked at him with some irritation and then said sternly: "The promise *was*—[*laughter*] "—there would be no question and answer period that I was to come in and say hello and beat it and get back to bed." It was obvious that Ford meant it. There was a long silence and, all over the room, faces fell. "However," said Ford quickly, " a couple of quick questions—if I can answer them. Shoot!"

Q :   *"Do you believe that filmmaking is more a matter of instinct than . . ."*
"Oh, definitely. *Anybody* can direct a picture once they know the fundamentals. Directing is not a mystery, it's not an art. The main thing about motion

pictures is: photograph the people's eyes. Photograph their eyes." He gestured to his chest and said: "Everything is from here up.

"You see, we have these instant geniuses now in the business, and they're all overcome with gimmicks—these gadgets, this camera, this wonderful-looking monster. And so they move it here, up, down, all over, so you get seasick."

"I went out to watch a couple of friends of mine doing *Hogan's Heroes*—John Banner and Werner Klemperer—and they had a new director there, and he moved the camera here, then the camera went up, then he moved over, then he went down, then it went up and he shot down at 'em. Meanwhile, he didn't watch the actors, didn't look at the actors *once*. Along about the tenth take he says: 'That's great! Print it.' And one of the actors says: 'I missed two lines in that,' and the director says: 'Oh, it doesn't make any difference.' And a German actor, who was supposed to speak with a German accent—by this time he'd lost the German accent and was speaking pure English. But the director wasn't watching that.

"But forget about the camera. Get a good cameraman—he knows more about a camera than you'll *ever* know—and say: 'I want to get So-and-So and So-and-So in, and I want it very close, because I'm not going to shoot any close-ups in here. If I shoot close-ups, I'm going to move one group here and one there so I can take individuals.' But get a good cameraman and work with your people. Look at their faces. See their eyes. You can express more with your eyes than you can with anything else. And that's about all."

Ford then noticed a girl in the front row and said to her: "How about you going into pictures? Hm? You're a good type." To the audience he said: "She'd photograph very well. What a shame I've retired."

Q: *"We heard that you were working on a new picture."*
"Well, not actually. I'm supervising the story of Chesty Puller, who was our most famous Marine, the most decorated Marine in history. I'm not actually directing it, I'm supervising it—nobody's *directing* it, we're just putting it together. I did go back to V.M.I. and Washington and Lee to do some scenes back there. We went back to do Robert E. Lee's tomb, where Chesty goes to say goodbye to him."

Ford's voice took a more personal tone as he added: "Chesty's a very dear friend of mine. We were in Korea together, and he kept me out of harm." Almost to himself, he added: "All I did was lose an eye.

"He's a very close friend of mine, and a great guy, and the greatest Marine the world has ever known. And I'm sort of supervising it. The Marine Corps sent over a lot of new material to us that has never been shown—I mean, real battle stuff that they've never given to the news weeklies or anybody else, because they thought at the time it was too—not too horrible—but, I mean, you see boys falling and that sort of thing. The real attacks. And then. . . ." And here Ford began going off into a private revery again, almost forgetting the audience. ". . . I got some great stuff when we were chased off the reservoir, during the blizzard. I had a camera—I photographed that—in a real blizzard, and . . . I just opened the camera wide open, and it came out beautifully. Have the retreat from the reservoir . . ."

"I hope we can get a print of that to show down here," said Father Frost. *"This Is Korea?"*

"No, the, uh . . ."

"Oh! . . . Oh, you can get it, as soon as we finish. It takes a long time, y'know, to get all this footage. I don't want too much war stuff in it. I want to make more of a human story about Chesty. Because he's a wonderful guy. I would like to make it his personal story. I don't want it filled with war stuff. I mean, the war stuff will be brief and to the point."

In the back of the room, a bearded, shaggy-haired ex-Marine from UCLA ("UCLA—that figures," said Ford later) stood up. "Is it true," he said, "that Chesty Puller tried to trade in three Navy Crosses for a Congressional Medal of Honor?"

"No," said Ford disgustedly. "He has *five* Navy Crosses." [*Laughter*] "No, that isn't true at all. That isn't true. But he wasn't made Commandant of Marines because he was too tough, and by that time everything was softening up. No, that is not true at all. Chesty should have received the Medal of Honor. He deserved it. But he does have five Navy Crosses. But as far as him politicking for a Congressional Medal of Honor, that isn't true at all. I don't know where you get that story."

"He's an ex-Marine and probably heard some scuttlebutt," called out a helpful soul from the audience.

Someone else began to ask a question, but Ford turned back to the ex-Marine. "What—were you—did you serve in Korea or in World War Two?" asked Ford.

"No, after that—I stood Chesty Puller's last inspection," said the ex-Marine.

"Well, don't you agree that he was a great guy?" said Ford.

"Uh . . ." [*Laughter*] "I did then, yes."

"Yeah. Well, he still is. And I'll bet he knew you by your first name—Cecil, or Cyril, or whatever your name is." [*Laughter*] "He was a great guy and he took care of his men." Then, almost to himself again, Ford added: "He took care of everybody but me . . ."

Q: *"How do you make your Westerns look so authentic, so real?"*

"Instinct again, I guess. I *have* been a cowboy and I punched cows for awhile. The boss's daughter, believe it or not, fell in love with me. She was six-foot-two and weighed about 210 pounds . . ." [*Laughter*] ". . . so I stole a horse and rode away . . ." [*Laughter*] ". . . and came to California." [*Laughter*] "But I *have* been a cowboy and I know the West pretty well."

Q: *"Did you run out of money when you were making* The Searchers? *A critic wrote at the time that you ran out of money."*

"That's partly true. They start bearing down—on every picture, towards the finish, they start bearing down on you. That's why the ends of pictures are not as good as the beginnings. 'Hurry it up, hurry it up!' You know, you're overbudget and everything. And this was—that's partly true."

Q: *"Do you think it hurt the picture?"*

"No, I don't think so. I didn't pay any attention to them. I gave them an evasive answer." [*Laughter*].

Ford answered another brief question, then graciously took his leave. As he stepped down from the podium, he gestured to his lapel, on which rested his DKA fraternity pin. Then he stretched out his arm and waved a last farewell.

John Ford Talks to Philip Jenkinson about Not Being Interested in Movies

PHILIP JENKINSON/1970

PHILIP JENKINSON: *Were you interested in movies way back?*
JOHN FORD: Not really—not interested in them now actually. It's a way of making a living.

J: *Was filmmaking in 1917 as primitive as everyone suggests?*
F: I hardly think that "primitive" is the right word. We had no lights and we had a big stage—just a board and over that we stretched cambric cotton to hold the light off—and there'd be five or six companies working side by side. We thought it was rather nice. We all knew one another and visited back and forth. We'd go over to the actors and say, "Do you mind coming over and playing a butler for us?" Well, not a butler—we didn't have butlers in those days: they were mostly Westerns.

J: *When did you become interested in Westerns?*
F: When I left school I went to college and didn't like it. So I left and worked in Arizona as a cowboy, and eventually ended up in Hollywood. I like to make Western pictures because I like to get out and live in the open: you get up early, you work late, you eat dinner with an appetite, you sleep well, and I do like the people you meet and work with. That is really my only interest in Westerns. As story material I am not particularly fascinated by them. It's not my metier by any means. None of my so-called better pictures are Westerns.

From *The Listener,* December 2, 1970.

J :   *What do you remember of* The Lost Patrol, *made in 1934?*

F :   We had one of the first of the so-called "producers" on this picture. We had a shot where the British cavalry were supposed to come to the rescue and it was very hard. When it was time to come on, this airplane flew over their heads and of course the horses scattered. The plane finally landed in a little satellite airfield they had, and this idiot producer got out with a big cigar. Of course it spoiled the shot for that day and we had to wait until the next day. He said to me: "Jack, I've been looking over your schedule. You start working at seven, then you quit at eleven, and start working at 2:30 or three. Look at those hours you're losing. If you worked right on through, you'd finish five or six days ahead."

I said: "Cliff, you can't work in this heat."

He said: "It's wonderful, I love it. It's great."

I said: "I'm sorry, I've got to line this shot up," and he wandered away. We finally got the shot and I said, "Where's Mr. So-and-So? Yes, the so-called producer who flew in last night."

"We've just taken him to the hospital with sunstroke."

J :   *There's a story that on the film* Wee Willie Winkie, *after the death of Victor McLaglen, you spontaneously suggested that they include a funeral scene.*

F :   Well, we were out there and I said: "It's a mistake in the story to kill McLaglen off, because he's one of the leading characters, but at least if we're going to kill him off, let's give him a funeral." It was in the rain, so I said, "Let's shoot it in the rain." Which we did. That's all there is to it. Just enough to fill in a day's work.

J :   *It looks like a sequence that would have taken a week to shoot, and instead you tell me you did it all in a day.*

F :   Oh no, we didn't do it in a day. Nothing of the sort. We did it in about an hour and a quarter.

J :   Stagecoach *was the first time you filmed in Monument Valley. Why did you decide to shoot there?*

F :   I used to stay occasionally with the chap who ran the trading post, and he said, "You know, the Navajos are starving. I understand you're going to do a Western. If you come up there and do it, you'd probably save a lot of lives." I think we left about $500,000 there. A man that rode a horse, if he provided his own horse, got ten dollars a day, the women got five dollars, and the children got three dollars a day. It put them on their feet and they appreciated it. If anybody else tries to come in there, they object. They don't want anybody in there but me.

J : *Do you see the systematic destruction of the Red Indian as something inevitable, or a blot on American history?*
F : That's a political question. I don't think it has anything to do with pictures. All I could say is "No comment." I wasn't alive then, I had nothing to do with it. My sympathy is all with the Indians. Do you consider the invasion of the Black and Tans in Ireland a blot on English history? Being Irish, it's my prerogative to answer a question with a question. Do you consider that a blot on English history?

J : *I don't know enough about it.*
F : It's the same thing.

J : *Can you tell me about the incredible story of your filming of the* Battle of Midway?
F : What was incredible about it?

J : *You running out there with a camera under direct attack.*
F : I did what?

J : *You were making shots and directing shots while the place was literally being blasted to bits.*
F : That was what I was getting paid for. There's nothing extraordinary about that. I was on this turret to report the position and the numbers of Japanese planes to the officers who were fifty feet under the ground, and meanwhile I had a little 16mm camera. I just reported the different things and took the pictures. That was what the Navy was for. What else could you do?

J : *In between making "A" pictures, you turned out scores and scores of "B" films.*
F : One of the troubles with directors is that they make a big picture—which might be a hit—and then they try to top it. And they usually fall flat on their faces. So I try to make it as a rule: if I make a big picture which is a hit I do a

cheap picture next. Relax for three or four weeks while preparing another story. Usually, of course, to my mind the little picture is better. My favorite picture, for example, is one you've never heard of called *The Sun Shines Bright*.

J :   *What aspects of American society at this moment dismay you the most?*
F :   I'm worried about these riots, these students. I'm worried about this anti-racism (sic). It doesn't mean the Negroes are doing it. They're being influenced by outside. Some other country. They are agents, the people who are doing things, that are being arrested . . . and the poor Negroes are getting the blame. That's why I think our ancestors would be . . . bloody ashamed of us if they saw us now. But things will get better.

J :   *Your films often depict bloodshed, yet I get the feeling you hate violence.*
F :   I do, and my pictures do not always show violence. Very, very few of them do. And if they show violence, it's over quickly. I suggest it more than anything else. I hate violence in pictures just as I do all this sex and incest and all the things that are going on now.

Ford on the Lido

DEREK MALCOLM/1971

I WAS SURPRISED TO be accorded an interview. John Ford was not fond of critics, though sometimes behoven to them. Perhaps since this was the August 1971 Venice Film Festival, where a special retrospective had been mounted, supervised by Peter Bogdanovich, he relented. But I still knocked on the door of his suite at the Excelsior Hotel on the Lido with some trepidation. What could I possibly ask him that he hadn't been asked before? But the fact that I had once been a jockey, and knew a bit about horses, might stand me in good stead. Ford might even think me a human being rather than a critic.

His wife answered the door, looking worried. She said she was terribly sorry but that they'd both come down with a bug, and John was in a worse state than she. It didn't look as if an interview was possible, though I could try later. Just as I was about to withdraw, I heard a voice coming from the general direction of the bathroom. It said, loud and clear, "Come on in. I can deal with two shits at once!"

Mrs. Ford raised her eyes to heaven and let me in. And Ford, then an old man, trundled in and said, "You English?" "No," I said, "I'm Scots." "Oh," he said, "That's better. . . . (pause) . . . What yer wanna know?" Horses, I thought to myself, horses.

"Well," I said, "I've always wondered where you got the horses for your Westerns." "Not from Scotland, that's for sure," said Ford, but, warming to the unexpectedly unintellectual question, "They have to be specially

---

Printed by permission of the author.

trained. Most of the actors can't ride them properly. They have to be quiet as hell."

"What about John Wayne?" I ventured gingerly. "Duke?" he said, possibly half joking, "We have to dope them for him."

The "interview" lasted an hour and a half, with intervals where Ford dealt summarily with one "shit" in the main room and several in the bathroom. He liked the idea of talking to a jockey. But when I came to write it up, there wasn't an awful lot of substance to it, though much entertainment. And *The Guardian,* where I was a critic, hadn't the sense of humor, or of Ford, to print it. Not even on the racing pages.

A Very Special Tribute to a Very Special Guy

KAY GARDELLA/1971

DIRECTOR JOHN FORD MIGHT not have invented either the Western or that ambulatory national monument, John Wayne, but most movie-goers think he created both, and it's far too late to try to change anybody's mind.

Now seventy-six and mending from a broken hip, Ford possibly would rather be remembered for such classic films as *The Informer,* but the tribute he'll be paid on CBS-TV tonight will further weld him to the saddle-and-saloon school of movie-making.

Called *The American West of John Ford,* the hour-long show will star his three favorite horsebackers—Duke Wayne, Jimmy Stewart, and Henry Fonda—and, in a brief bedside segment filmed in his Bel Air, Calif., home, the wry and sometimes irascible Old Man himself.

"There are no creative people at the head of studios any more," he said while sitting upright in bed, a half-spent cigar clenched between his teeth. "Pictures are being controlled from Madison Avenue and Wall Street. Darryl F. Zanuck is the only movie maker left, and he's out now. I feel very sad, particularly when it's a business I love. Still, you remain here, always hoping that someday it will come back and be the industry it once was."

Ford shifted his weight and tried to find a more comfortable spot for his aching hip.

"I'm a student of history," he continued. "I like the Western because it's

From the *New York Sunday News,* Section 2, December 5, 1971. © 1971 the *New York Daily News, L.P.* Reprinted by permission.

made on location. But there's a sameness about them. There's always the same old church, the same old shootout, two doubles in a saloon faking a fight and the same old Western town."

A TV set rested at the foot of Ford's bed. He said he doesn't like television and rarely has it on.

"All I watch is baseball," he said. "TV doesn't interest me. Most of the shows I've seen I don't like. They're done in too much of a hurry. They don't have endings. As for movies, they're all cut to pieces. Particularly my own. They're massacred! That's why I don't watch my movies on TV. Anyway, I don't like to watch movies. I like to make them."

Ford's home is a sort of Western museum—a pair of gloves worn by Buffalo Bill in his Wild West shows, a war bonnet from the Battle of the Little Big Horn, and a prominently displayed bumper sticker which reads: "God Loves John Wayne."

John Ford loves the big guy, too. Wayne, in Ford's opinion, is the No. 1 star in movies today. The two men are close friends and have worked together many times. It figures, since Ford is a man's man, a reputation he thoroughly enjoys. He readily admits a preference for films about men in a man's world, but he's not anti-women, as some critics have implied.

In fact, he said, his Oscar-winning film, *The Quiet Man,* belonged as much to Maureen O'Hara as it did to John Wayne, the picture's leading man.

"My leading ladies all liked me," he said with more than a trace of pride.

What does John Ford think of John Ford?

The director smiled and rubbed his hand across the stubble on his chin. "I prefer to think of myself as a hard-nosed, hard-working director with a sense of humor and no temper, temperament, or inhibitions."

Yes, John Ford Knew a Thing or Two about Art

LARRY SWINDELL/1973

HE SAID HE WAS pleased that I wasn't scribbling a lot of notes while we talked. That always bothered the hell out of him, because it deprived a meeting of its personal side and he preferred doing things on a personal basis.

"If I say something worth remembering, you will," John Ford said, "and if it isn't memorable, why bother to write it down?"

He loathes tape recorders, too, but would permit them among friends. "Now that they've decided my work belongs to the ages, they try to get me to talk about it. I don't enjoy that, and it has been my humor to spend my time doing things I enjoy. But they're going to quote me anyway, so I help see they get it right." I told him a tape recorder wasn't my style.

He showed me a compact little book called simply "John Ford," then newly published in England but authored by a young American critic named Peter Bogdanovich, apparently esteemed by Ford as both friend and disciple. America's most honored film director was obviously proud of the book with its eloquent anthology of stills from his movies.

Yet he tried to conceal his pleasure. They'd been lacquering him with praise for most of his long lifetime but he hadn't adjusted to the odor. He was still embarrassed by fame, and a gruff scorn of praise had become part of the public John Ford.

He was pleased, too, that I had already heard of Peter Bogdanovich, who

From the *Philadelphia Inquirer,* September 16, 1973. 8–10. © 1973 the *Philadelphia Inquirer.* Reprinted by permission from The Philadelphia Inquirer.

he said was making his own first picture. He said Peter had what most of the early directors but few of the later ones had: "A pure love for the activity of making pictures." The words were slow and careful, and emphasis on the word activity told me it was a conscious substitute for the customary "business" or "art."

Yes, John Ford said he knew a thing or two about art. He spelled it with a capital F.

That was five years ago. I had met John Ford twice, but many years earlier. He obviously wouldn't remember me, so I made no reference. The previous contacts had been sort of official, but this was the first and only "personal" meeting and I felt lucky in having the invitation. Ford, who was then seventy-three, had not been "giving interviews" for several years and would devote his idle time to his pals or to himself only. But something in a letter I'd written had won his confidence and interest.

He was glad someone with "a good feeling" about the movies was doing a biography of Spencer Tracy. His secretary telephoned that I could have an hour with Mr. Ford in his Beverly Hills office. The hour grew into a complete afternoon. I didn't overstay; we were just enjoying ourselves. Besides, he said, "I don't have a damn thing to do except just be here and refuse visitors. I think I'm retired now. I may never make another picture, much as I'd like to. I'm too old and blind and tired."

One eye had been covered by a black patch for several years, and vision in the other was suspect. When he read, it was with great effort and his nose almost touched the print. But even twenty years earlier he had looked somehow ancient, and perhaps only his refusal to compromise being comfortable had allowed him to endure. He was the raffish prize in an otherwise impeccable office—wearing a battered cap, gray tweed jacket, green polo shirt, white corduroy slacks, and dirty white tennis shoes.

I had been warned he could be impatiently mean, but things went well from the start. I noted the niceness of Dixie, his secretary, and Ford said she was a Texican and they're good people. I said I was a native Texan and that got him going.

Really? From where? I said a little town called Quanah at the southeast tip of the Panhandle, near the Red River. He'd been there and had slept overnight in the Crawford Hotel that I assured him was still there. He was delighted that I was a "Texican" with a faint trace of Comanche blood, and from a town named for one of his heroes.

"Quanah Parker was a remarkable chief and a great American. Ford reflected, "who finally saw that the white man would have to be accommodated. If you can't lick 'em, join 'em. Of course, he was half white, but you knew that already."

Yes, the saga of the Parker family was folklore back home. John Ford and I reviewed almost-matching versions of Cynthia Ann Parker's extraordinary tragic life: taken at six by Comanches who massacred the rest of a Texas settlement; growing up as squaw to Chief Nocona and mother to Quanah before her recapture by the Cavalry many years later; then imprisoned with white eastern relatives, pining in her old age for the warrior son who became the architect of peace between his two peoples.

"I always intended to make a picture about Quanah Parker. I discussed a script first with Dudley Nichols and then Lamar Trotti, but the war came and that diverted us. There's a fictional suggestion of Cynthia Ann in *The Searchers* but it's hardly the same.

"Now take *Cheyenne Autumn*. It was very disappointing to me in a personal way, because I couldn't get inside a whole tribe of people. But if you can get inside a Quanah Parker, he can represent the tribe. But I'd say you're going to have to make the picture."

He never said movie, or film: it was always picture—the term most often employed by Hollywood oldtimers for whom moviemaking was a primarily visual adventure.

We talked about his work and I held my own, even showed off a bit; and he was flattered that I didn't just carry on over *Stagecoach* and *The Informer* and *The Grapes of Wrath*. My own favorites in the Ford inventory included such relative obscurities as *Steamboat 'Round the Bend, They Were Expendable,* and *The Prisoner of Shark Island,* and I could tell he was pleased, as well as grateful to be talking with someone whose liking for pictures wasn't impressively intellectual.

He said *The Sun Shines Bright* was his favorite job and that surprised me until he clarified that he was talking about what he liked, not what he thought was best. "When they ask me what I consider is my best picture, I often say *Stagecoach* if I answer at all, because it usually shuts them up without an argument. Hell, I don't know what could make one picture best or even better. I don't have that kind of mind."

He protested that his intelligence was only ordinary, but that if he'd been smarter perhaps he wouldn't have become "this great director you keep hearing about." I didn't ask, but he identified Claire Trevor in *Stagecoach* as "possibly the best actress I worked with, or as good as any . . . so true in performance as to be almost overlooked." Then he smacked his lips for emphasis. "But the best actor I worked with was the one you're writing about. You are here to talk about Spence, aren't you?"

I was, and we did. What made the meeting so vital was that John Ford alone had brought Spencer Tracy into the talkies—obstinately, because nobody at Fox wanted to take on a stage actor not endowed with conventional good looks. When the Tracy biography was published, some reviewers cited Ford's memoir of *Up the River* 1930 as an especially satisfying passage. Here it's reprised in condensed form, John Ford talking:

"The Fox executives sent me to New York to assess the new plays and scout young actors. I needed a male lead for *Up the River;* it was my next assignment and a prison picture, so on my first night in town I saw a prison play—*The Last Mile* with Spencer Tracy as Killer Meers.

"I liked it so much that I went back the next night, and was tantalized by Spence. I began to see that he had it all—the consummate power of an actor. So, hell, I went a third time, and introduced myself to Spence backstage. He took me to the Lambs Club for what turned out to be quite an evening.

"We stayed until about four o'clock when I think they threw us out. Most of the time we only talked baseball, but I liked Spence so much I knew I had to have him in my next picture, whether it was *Up the River* or something else. The way it turned out, I was supposed to see six plays in six nights but I saw *The Last Mile* every night I was there.

"Spence had tested for several studios but nobody wanted him. They said he was ugly. But I had an ornery streak, and Fox gave in. *Up the River* turned out all right and Spence was perfect. Unlike most stage-trained actors, he instinctively subdued himself before a camera. And he was as natural as if he didn't know a camera was there.

"We didn't work together again until *The Last Hurrah* almost thirty years later. But I always wanted him—he was everybody's first choice. Once Irving Thalberg agreed to loan Spence to me for *The Plough and the Stars,* but then Irving died, and just about that time Tracy was becoming an important M-G-M star and that bastard Mayer reneged on our deal.

"When I say Spencer Tracy was the best actor we ever had, I'm giving you something of my philosophy of acting. The best is the most natural. Scenery never got chewed in my pictures. I prefer actors who can just be. That's why I consider John Wayne a good actor for pictures, although he would be deficient on any stage. And that's why I put together my own stock company for people to joke about. I used my friends in pictures because I like an atmosphere in which people can work well together. Besides, I knew what they could do, and I don't coach acting. I don't even understand it, the way George Cukor and John Cromwell understand acting.

"George Stevens can take an ordinary performance and edit it into a brilliant one, the way a good newspaperman trims a reporter's story to make it read better. I admire that, but for me the orgasm of picture-making is yelling the final 'Cut!' Then I'm ready to start a new project, and someone else can edit my last job."

Dixie had gone home, the sun had gone down outside and I sensed that my host was tiring. I got up from my chair to do the decent thing but I was rudely commanded to sit back down, while John Ford reflected.

"The simple fact is, my interest is pictorial. As a small boy I liked to draw and had a kind of talent for composition.

"I was a kid out of high school and the movies and Hollywood were both very new. My older brother Francis was established in pictures so I joined him. I did some camera work and, sometimes, a little writing. There were no unions, it was a carefree activity, and I was nineteen when I directed my first two-reeler.

"Well, pictures have changed a lot. Most of today's so-called film criticism baffles me and we have too many critics who lack affinity for public taste. But I try not to grumble, for I was fortunate to work in a field that was young and raw and new.

"Sure, I took a lot of crap from studio types. I compromised. But it wasn't like today when the motion picture industry is too goddam big and complicated. On comparative terms I had a lot of freedom, and I had a hell of a lot of fun making pictures and that was important.

"They ask if I believe in the future of motion pictures and I say yes because I do. But not so eloquently as I believe in their past."

Then he studied me with one moist eye and said, "Now tell me where we've met before, for I know we have."

Surprised, I told him that about fifteen years earlier I had twice contacted him on behalf of The Great Films Society, an early study group of which I was a member while still in my teens, and with all my hair.

He had consented to be our guest for the inevitable panel discussions following screenings of first The Iron Horse, and then The Lost Patrol. He was curious that I had not referenced our background, and I was embarrassed. And about then, I took my leave.

When the book was published, I mailed a copy to John Ford, with a message of gratitude inscribed in large characters to facilitate his reading it. I never heard from him. The next time I was in Los Angeles I resisted an urge to call on him again, for I had no reason to see him other than admiration, and feared a turn-down.

Now I regret such reticence. About a year ago one of my friends from the film colony said he had happened to mention my name during whatever business he was conducting with that grand old Irishman, and John Ford had said that he and I are real good pals.

Well, my pal died a couple of weeks ago. He was born Sean O'Feeney, the youngest of thirteen children, in Maine; but sixty of his seventy-eight years were spent in Hollywood where he adopted the professional surname of his older brother. He mastered his craft in silent pictures and became the foremost director of the prewar talkies. Afterward his reputation declined until critics in the '60s Film Generation decided, against his scoffing, that any John Ford movie had an extra dimension that made it timeless.

Perhaps he was America's greatest movie director, or perhaps he was merely what he said he was—an overrated technician with some talent for composition. I have some talent for memory, and I'm going to give John Ford the best of it. He gave me a full afternoon out of one glorious life.

One More Hurrah

WALTER WAGNER/1973

IN THE BEDROOM ON Copa de Ora Road in Bel Air, Ford, in green pajamas, looked like a pixyish pirate. The famous black patch over his left eye was in place (to protect it from daylight). He'd been home from the hospital for only three days following surgery for the cancer that would soon kill him. This was the last interview of his life.

Because of his visitor's last name, Ford assumed he was German. *Herr Wagner, wie geht es Ihnen?* he rattled off in excellent German. Luckily, his visitor did speak German. After several other amenities and polite small talk in German, the conversation switched to English.

"I should offer you a drink. This is gin and stout."

"No, thank you. I don't drink."

"Well, neither do I. But the doctor ordered this to put on weight. It tastes and smells horrible, but I have to drink two before dinner."

"It looks like root beer."

"Oh, God, now you've killed it for me."

"Sorry."

I've never written a book about my life because it's been too complicated. I have written articles. I have even written short stories. I will confess they are children's stories, but the idea of sitting down and writing a book is rather beyond me. My grandson contemplates doing it. I wouldn't have the pa-

From *You Must Remember This.* Putnam: New York, 1975. 45–54. © 1975 by Walter Wagner. Used by permission of G. P. Putnam's Sons, a division of Penguin Putnam, Inc.

tience, though on second thought if I told the truth it probably would be very exciting. But the truth about my life is nobody's damn business but my own. Perhaps I should amplify. I've done so many things, been so many places, that I'm afraid an autobiography would be too episodic. And there are certain things in my life that I would like to forget. I didn't murder anybody or rob anybody but I got mixed up in a couple of revolutions and that sort of thing. . . .

My father came to this country to fight. *You* can call it the Civil War, but my wife is from South Carolina, so we call it the War Between the States in this house. My father had two brothers and a brother-in-law. One was in the Confederate Army, and two were in the Union Army. When he arrived, the war was over. I asked him once, "Which side were you going to fight for?" And he answered, "Either side."

My wife's father was a Confederate, and both her grandfathers were Confederate colonels. Sherman burned her house down. She wasn't alive at the time, of course. But she was brought up on those stories. I had two uncles in the Union Army and one in the Confederate Army. In deference to my wife, I keep quiet about the ones in the Union Army. If you go down to the library, you will see a regimental flag that was made about the time of Appomattox. It came down to my wife. It's a very faint, very old Confederate flag. Ask my daughter Barbara to show it to you. She is a student of history, but it's all Louis XIV, XV and XVI. Right now she's on a Henry VIII kick.

As a kid I was fascinated by the nickelodeons of that period. Any time I got a nickel or a dime I would go to the movies.

How did I get to Hollywood? By train. Oh, you mean *why* did I come to Hollywood? I had a brother who was quite a considerable star in the film world, Francis Ford. I decided to follow him out here because I was at the University of Maine on an athletic scholarship and I didn't make it. I think I was there about eight or twelve days, I forget which. Incidentally, about an hour ago I received a letter from them asking if they could name their School of Dramatic Arts after me. I'm going to tell them to go ahead. It's a great honor.

I remember the last night on the train. I was coming tourist, and I had to go without dinner because I had no money in my pocket. So I arrived penniless, as the expression goes.

I started my career as a ditchdigger. In other words, I got a job on the labor gang at Universal when Carl Laemmle, Sr., was running the studio. Then my brother made me an assistant propman. I then became an assistant director.

How I became a director is a long story, but if you have the time, I'll tell it to you.

There was a big party one night for Carl Laemmle at the studio. There were seventy-five to one hundred guests, all very important, most of them from the East. They had never seen a studio before. The assistant directors, of which I was one, and the propmen acted as bartenders. We worked all night and managed to get an hour's sleep, or a half hour's sleep, under the bar. We still had to show up for work at eight thirty in the morning. But none of the directors showed up. I was on my set on the back lot, and my director hadn't shown up either. They were all sleeping it off.

Isadore Bernstein, the general manager of the studio, was a very fine man, a very dear friend of mine. As a matter of fact, he was the best man at my wedding. He came riding up on his little pinto horse and said, "For God's sake, Jack, do something, Mr. Laemmle and all his guests are coming down here, and they want to see some action. I can't find any of our directors. You'll have to direct something. This is the only set with riders, extras and so forth."

I asked him what I should do.

He was frantic, and he said, "Do anything! Show them some action!"

I thought, What the hell can I do? By the time Laemmle and his guests showed up I had an idea. I told the cowboys—I think I had about twelve of them—to come riding through the street, whooping and yelling, and to shoot at the buildings, then to pull up at a hitching post, turn around and ride back again. They did it all great.

Mr. Bernstein came up and said, "That's fine. Do something else."

"What the hell more can I do?"

He said, "Mr. Laemmle's guests are all thrilled and fascinated. They have never seen horsemen, cowboys before."

I told him I'd try to think of something. I went up to the cowboys and said, "When I fire a shot, I want two of you fellows to fall." In those days they got two dollars for a fall. Now it would be about two hundred and fifty. So they came whooping down the street again, and I fired a shot. And all twelve of them fell off their horses. I thought that was a little incongruous, a little stupid, one shot felling twelve men.

Mr. Bernstein came riding up again, and I told him, "I didn't want that. I only wanted two or three to fall."

He said, "Oh, that's great. They don't know the difference. That's fine. Keep it in. Is it in the can?"

I said yes.

Then he said, "Now do something else."

I told him I had run out of ideas.

"Oh, you'll think of something. I'll go back and talk to Mr. Laemmle and his guests and keep them busy. You go ahead and think of something spectacular for the cowboys to do."

I was stumped. What could I do on that street? It was just a makeshift street, with wooden buildings and false fronts. Then I had a brilliant idea, or at least at that time I thought it was brilliant. In the natural course of the story we were shooting—I forget the name of the film now—the saloon was supposed to catch fire and burn down. It was a cheap street, and I thought why not burn the whole goddamn street down?

I had all the buildings set afire, and I told the cowboys that this time I wasn't going to pay them for all falling unless I specified it. So they rode down the street again, shooting and yelling while it burned.

Mr. Bernstein said, "Gosh, that was great."

I said, "You asked for something spectacular." Then I told him I was really out of ideas.

Mr. Bernstein said, "Well, I'll get Mr. Laemmle's guests away and we'll try to find another set whose director isn't drunk so we can show them something else."

"Thank God," I said.

I gave orders to put the fire out and stop the cameras. When Laemmle and his guests left, I was exhausted.

The aftermath of this was that it looked so good on the screen that they enlarged that little two-reel picture into a five-reeler. It turned out to be a very exciting picture. About four months later Harry Carey, who was an important silent star, needed a director for one of his Westerns.

Mr. Laemmle said, "Let Jack Ford direct it. He yells good."

So I became a director, and I was scared to death. But Harry was a very dear and very close friend and remained so until his death. Harry helped me immeasurably. Then I directed another picture from a story I had written, and I do remember the name of this one. It was called *The Sky Pilot*.

I don't know how many films I've made. Peter Bogdanovich, who did an article about me, the son of a bitch, I think he added them up and there were a hundred and thirty-two. I call Bogdanovich a son of a bitch because his article was inaccurate in many ways. He had me talking out of the side of my mouth in very bad vernacular. After all, I did major in English, and I'm from New England, and I am proud of my accent and very particular about my grammar. He had me practically speaking argot. He wrote the article with my permission, and he was going to expand it into a book. But he did not get my permission for that.

Frankly, I remember none of my silent pictures with any warmth. They were all hard work. My first silent hit, if I may use that expression, was *The Iron Horse*. It was a great epic of its time. I think it grossed seven million three hundred thousand some odd dollars. That was an astounding figure for those days.

I had no difficulty whatever making the transition from silents to talkies. By the way, neither did John Gilbert. John actually had a very good, resonant voice. He'd been an actor on the stage, and he knew his business. He did a talkie, *Queen Christina,* with Greta Garbo. Then he stayed off the screen for a while and died. But that thing about him having a weak voice is untrue. He had a good voice.

That story about Victor McLaglen being drunk when he starred in *The Informer* is an ill-founded rumor. It is actually a libelous statement. There is an axiom in the picture business that nobody under the influence of alcohol can play a drunk. And I believe that. All the famous drunks that we have in the picture business and the people who play drunks are teetotalers when they work. You can't play a drunk while you are under the influence. Victor had to run too many gamuts of emotion, bravado, nervousness, fear, sometimes all in one scene, and go back to bravado again and resume the whole thing. He had too much to do to take a drink. He had some very tough lines. After all, he was not an Irishman, and he was playing an Irishman in this. He had to assume an Irish accent, which he did splendidly. It is untrue, absolutely untrue, that he was drunk while we were shooting.

I was surprised when *The Informer* won an Academy Award. You don't just pick up a story, do a picture of it, and say this is an Academy Award picture. I chose it because it was a very good, very sound and substantial story, a good character story.

Stagecoach was a typical Western, lots of emotion, lots of action, although at that time it was slightly out of line. I mean, the girl who played the lead was a prostitute. The boy, John Wayne, was an escaped convict. In those days you didn't do that sort of thing. But it had a happy ending, and that's probably why I liked it.

As it turned out, I received no criticism because I broke new ground with *Stagecoach*. But I got a lot of followers, copiers.

I had no special approach to *The Grapes of Wrath*. Darryl Zanuck called me in and just told me to go out and make it. He was the boss. And I was under contract to Fox at the time.

It had a good story, too. It was a story I was in sympathy with. I was born on a farm. We weren't rich or really comfortable or well-to-do. Because I was pinching poverty while I was growing up, I had complete sympathy with these people.

It was just another job to be done to the best of my ability. I didn't wave any magic wand or look into a crystal ball. I just went out and did it. It was a lot of fun because I was back working again with Henry Fonda, really one of my favorite actors, really my favorite actor. Why is he my favorite actor? That's a stupid question, isn't it? I will answer the best I can without being rude. Because he is a great and immensely talented performer.

I finished *Grapes of Wrath* under budget and turned it in. With Darryl I didn't have to worry about how it would be cut because he was a great cutter. The night I finished I got on my boat and started to sail to Honolulu. Before I left, I had a meeting with Darryl, and I said, "I think it's a good picture. It's meaty and down-to-earth But I think it needs a happier ending. I hate to see the picture end with Fonda walking across the dance hall and disappearing into the darkness. I think it should end with the mother."

He said, "That's a good idea. Let's think it over."

I sailed on the midnight tide. I was three days out and had a good forwarding breeze and I was at the wheel when a phone call came from Darryl.

"Listen to this," he said. "Listen to this scene I've written. I've looked at the picture twice since you left, and I agree with you that it needs a happier ending. It needs an ending of hope for the future. Listen to this carefully. Can you hear me?"

I told him we had a very good connection.

He read me the scene and asked if I wanted it rewritten.

I told him no, that it was great.

Then he said, "Who's going to direct it?"

I said, "Darryl, it's only a two-shot. I'd appreciate it if you went out and directed it yourself."

"Okay," he said, "I'd like to."

So he did it himself in one take. And they put it in as the end of the picture.

To use a familiar expression, Darryl is the last of the great tycoons. The last of the great operators, the last of the great executive producers. The man is really a genius. We've remained very close, very dear friends. As a matter of fact, I speak to Darryl more often than to many of my so-called friends out here. He calls from New York, and I haven't asked him what he's doing since he left Fox. I'm afraid to. It might break my heart.

I was at sea again when I heard that *The Grapes of Wrath* had won the Academy Award. Henry Fonda was with me, and he heard it on the radio. We were fishing. Henry is a great fisherman. As a matter of fact he's hooked on it. He's mad for fishing even though he never catches any fish.

I never went to an Academy Award ceremony. Why should I? I don't like those things.

If I do have a favorite picture, it goes back before *The Grapes of Wrath*. The picture I like to look at occasionally, even on television, is *Young Mr. Lincoln*. That I think is my favorite because it was a good picture and I liked Lincoln and I like a simple story.

I've always used a great deal of music in my pictures, although I don't have a good ear. I like country music, Western music. I go from the sublime to the ridiculous. I like classical music at times. I like your namesake, Herr Wagner.

I don't approve of some of the changes I've seen in Hollywood. I don't like pornography. I hate to go to a theater and look at pornography. I don't think it has any place on our screen. I think we made pictures better years ago than we are making them today.

The Quiet Man was made in my mother's and father's country, Connemara, Ireland. It was a lot of fun doing the picture. We got breaks on the weather, and when the weather wasn't particularly good, we still went out and took advantage of the bad weather. When the picture was shown in Ireland, all the critics were angry. They didn't like it. Every one of them came up with the same statement—that Mr. Ford had used a green filter on his camera to make the hills and the fields green. I really blew my top at them, and I had to laugh. I'd never heard of a green filter, and you can't use a filter on a Technicolor camera anyway. So I wrote each one of the critics a nice letter saying, If you would get out of that goddamn apartment and take a bus ride into the country, you would see that the hills of northern Ireland are green. But these stupid guys, these city dwellers living in Dublin, saying that I used a green filter—that really got my goat.

I have no idea why I have survived in this business. Luck, I guess. But I do believe in the American Dream. Definitely. Definitely. I think if you work hard enough, you will succeed.

To be quite blunt, I make pictures for money, to pay the rent. I do think that there is an art to the making of a motion picture. There are some great artists in the business. I am not one of them. I think Frank Capra is an artist. George Cukor is a great artist. So are George Stevens, George Sidney, and William Wellman. No, Wellman isn't an artist. He's just a goddamn good director.

A director can either make a film or can break it. He must be conversant with the subject. He must hypnotize himself to be sympathetic toward the subject matter. Sometimes we are not. Being under contract you make pictures that you don't want to make, but you try to steel yourself, to get enthused over them. You get on the set, and you forget everything else. You say these actors are doing the best they can. They also have to make a living. As a director I must help them as much as I can. I think a director can help an actor or an actress, and he can also help the cameraman, the electricians and everybody else. I think he brings a great deal to a film.

I want to thank you very much. People call and make appointments and ask if they can drop by. They are all friends. But if they're supposed to be here at three, they usually show up at five fifteen—so your entire day is helter-skelter. And so now I am not receiving any visitors. None of them are punctual, but you were punctual.

Walter, you asked me why I didn't write my autobiography, and I told you that I've led sort of a peculiar life. And I also told you that I was never arrested for anything. I haven't committed arson or petty larceny or anything of that sort, but during World War Two, for example, I was in the OSS. I've had a checkered career. I've alternated my life between motion pictures and the Navy. I retired as an admiral of the Navy. I think you know that.

During my spare time I've been mixed up in a lot of things. I've made tours of colleges and universities and spoke, not very well, but in a colloquial manner and tried to get some humor in it, tried not to make my talk dry as dust.

Maybe I've given you the wrong idea—that I'm wanted for murder in Minnesota—but I've done so many things and been so many places. There are no warrants out for me. I am just telling you that everybody thinks of a motion-picture director living in Bel Air or Beverly Hills in a big house with a lot of servants and driving a Rolls-Royce. But we do have other things to do while we're waiting for our next picture. I like to get out and travel.

I remember coming back from a trip once during the war, and I talked before this audience, and I was telling them about some of the strange places I'd visited for the OSS.

This very supercilious and sarcastic man came up to me and said, "Tell me, Commander Ford, when was the last time you were in Tibet?"

I said, "Exactly ten days ago, sir." He looked so sort of flabbergasted. Then he said, "I don't believe it." And I replied, "Screw you. It happens to be true."

I hope I haven't been abrupt with you. I hope I haven't been rude. You see, people have been asking me these questions for more than fifty years, and no one's yet come up with an original question.

You say someone's called me the greatest poet of the Western saga. I am not a poet, and I don't know what a Western saga is. I would say that is horseshit. I'm just a hard-nosed, hardworking, run-of-the-mill director.

INDEX